KV-354-680

THE ART OF COMMUNICATION
Communication in Industry

A. C. LEYTON

formerly Head of Department of Management and Social Sciences, Northampton College of Advanced Technology, (now City University) London

London: Sir Isaac Pitman and Sons Ltd.

First published 1968

SIR ISAAC PITMAN AND SONS LTD.

Pitman House, Parker Street, Kingsway, London, W.C.2.
Pitman House, Bouverie Street, Carlton, Victoria 3053,
Australia
P.O. Box 7721, Johannesburg, Transvaal, S. Africa
P.O. Box 6038, Portal Street, Nairobi, Kenya

PITMAN PUBLISHING CORPORATION
20 East 46th Street, New York, N.Y. 10017

SIR ISAAC PITMAN (CANADA) LTD.
Pitman House, 381-383 Church Street, Toronto

MADE IN GREAT BRITAIN AT THE PITMAN PRESS, BATH F8—(B. 648)

Contents

Definition—Sound Argument—Who Affirms Must Prove—What Must be Proved?—Argument by Induction—Argument by Analogy—Deductive Argument—Arguing from Effect to Cause—Arguing from Cause to Effect—Refutation of an Argument.

Sending People on a Course—An Education and Training Department—Considerations that Might Affect an Education and Training Policy—Possible Education and Training Courses.

Communication Theory—Insight and Knowledge—Communication and Attitudes—Organization—Creation—Sanctions—Understanding the Nature of Communication—Defined Language—Supervisory Practice—Line Management and Communication—Language—Meetings—Joint Consultation—Agenda and Minutes—Effective Speaking—Purposes of Speaking—Human Relations — Instructions — Letters — Reports — Interviewing — Delegation —Enthusiasm—Sound Argument—Modern Management.

Technical and commercial colleges and the art of communication.

Preface

"COMMUNICATION" is obviously something that can be discoursed upon at length, with definitions and conceptions warranting the devotion of profounder pages than might here appear. But this book has been designed to have a very limited field of application, and "communication" is less looked upon as a phenomenon basic to our lives than a practice of industry meriting special attention. Quite clearly, as is pointed out in Chapter 1 of the book, communication is so large a part of our lives that any attempt to engage in abstraction of it is most unsatisfying. We are always communicating; in fact we do so practically from birth. Experiments have proved that a person can scarcely endure being cut off from all communication with him over any long period.

Technological growth has been rapid over the past few years; where managers could rely on fairly simple literature applicable to their specialism, today information of all kinds has so increased that managers are hard put to it to absorb the information given to them. The literature pertaining to a specialism has itself so much increased, and so many countries are now involved, that someone has had to engage in a digest of information to meet the needs of busy practitioners.

This book has been written in an attempt to be helpful to the busy manager, who might neglect the best means of communication, not because he intends to do so, but because he is so busy. There are many men and women who became good friends and advisers to me. To this unnamed parade of friends I would offer deep obeisance. I salute them, and now have very pleasant memories to live with.

Dostoievsky, in *The Brothers Karamazov*, making allowance perhaps for poetic licence, said: "If people around you are spiteful and callous and will not hear you, fall down before them and beg their forgiveness; for in truth, you are to blame for their not wanting to hear you."

And John Locke said: "Were the instruments of language as the instruments of knowledge more thoroughly weighed, a great many other controversies that make such a noise in the world would of themselves cease."

Any thought given to the problem of communication will be helpful. It is one of the most puzzling problems of present day philosophy, as is shown by the extent of the literature devoted in recent years to its solution.

The chapters devoted to the meaning of communication, to communication in industry and to a restatement and summary (Chapters 1, 2 and 3) use a lot of paper. But I am concerned with problems of communication, and do not wish merely to repeat in detail conventions established in regard to the special forms of communication, such as talking, report-writing, interviewing and so on. I believe that the special forms of communication need not really be separately explained; they can, in fact, be deduced or inferred from the general principles of communication.

A book is judged by the intention governing it, more particularly having regard to the reader for whom it is written. This book was not prepared for academics—excellent people though they are—with whom, nevertheless, the good lecture is an exception rather than the rule, as long association with students of all kinds has confirmed; for the effective presentation of information does not sit easily on all shoulders. Authors such as Sir Ernest Gowers, Professor Ifor Evans, Professor R. O. Kapp and G. H. Vallins did not presumably write primarily for such persons. The opinions expressed by these writers would no doubt be known to academic lecturers, who probably learned all there was to know about these opinions in their formal education and training. I have not catered for their interests, nor do I seek their comments; in this book theoretical generalizations are down to a minimum.

I may at times be unconsciously imitating what many writers

have said about the use of appropriate language. These writers are numerous, and I owe to them a great deal that helped to develop my own interest. Failure to acknowledge them by name is not intentional, but it is difficult to remember whether an idea is original or has been borrowed from someone else. If the latter is the case, I apologize now.

Professor Kapp has argued the use of "functional" English, Dr. Ifor Evans has spoken of "direct" English, Sir Ernest Gowers has written on "simple" English. The puzzling fact remains that in spite of these very helpful writers there is still a tendency to write in turgid English. This fault can be coupled with bad thinking.

The book is intended for *industrial* readers, primarily for *managers*, who have the tiresome, everyday duty of communication with perhaps thousands of men. It has been designed for them with gratitude and even nostalgia, in deep appreciation of the hospitality, generosity and fun that attended my visits to different parts of the country.

My particular thanks are due to Dr. Bakke who (when he spoke, at least) was Director of the Labour and Management Centre of Yale University, to the Fourth Programme of T.W.I., and to the British Association for Commercial and Industrial Education (B.A.C.I.E.), particularly the latter, for the encouraging and provocative work I was able to do on meetings. Although Dr. Bakke and the Fourth Programme of T.W.I. were positive influences, both speaker and programme confirmed what I already believed. The fact remains, however, that both Dr. Bakke and the T.W.I. Fourth Programme were responsible initially for the direction my interests took. To them I am deeply grateful.

Some readers may have been in one or other of my audiences when I was lecturing; they may recognize some things I have said in my lectures. I ask their forgiveness, but it is impossible to think about a discipline without having certain basic ideas.

A.C.L.

1 The Meaning of Communication

A Chapter on the Nature of Effective Communication

THE importance of the problem of communication cannot be exaggerated. A tragedy of today is that it has been so long under-rated. After all, the very character and fortune of our lives are determined by our ability to communicate our ideas and our feelings, to stimulate reactions, and perhaps to receive and appraise the writing and talk of others.

The word "communication" has now come into fashion. It is quite a good word, and certainly preferable to the absurd term "self-expression." It really is foolish to think that a person need only express himself to be immediately understood by others. The word "communication" goes beyond the words "speaking" and "writing," to include all the aspects of verbal and unspoken or unwritten communication—for example, not only speaking and writing but gesture, layout, reading and listening. Industry calls for the skills not only of written and spoken words, but certainly the art of listening, which will be dealt with later.

To write about "communication" in the fullest sense of the term would be to discourse on life itself, for "communication" is at the very centre of our social lives. We are always communicating.

Definition

It may be necessary, however, to have a working definition of "communication." Obviously physicists, mathematicians, statisticians or novelists will each give a different meaning to the term. The meaning given to the term as here used is: *transmitting a message in order to evoke a discriminating response.* "Communication" does not merely mean *talking* to people, it also means, as we have just said, listening to them, listening being as much an act of communication as talking is. Unless we listen to people effectively we cannot really talk to them effectively.

"Communication" shall not mean merely conveying a message *without regard to eliciting the kind of response sought.* Certain salesmen might well emphasize the negative kind of response. Salesmen, for example, may not care about discerning or understanding response to advertisements. It is precisely because we do not set out in other circumstances to get a *discriminating* response or in setting out to get it do not always succeed in doing so, that there is a great deal of frustration on jobs and in relationships.

When we are in one another's drawing-rooms or in public bars we often talk only because it is bad manners to keep silent. A man standing at a public bar having a drink and not speaking is branded as a solitary drinker. He feels himself ostracized unless he allows noises to come out of his face. What he says may not matter; if anybody in a public bar or a drawing-room or in a railway compartment took shorthand notes of what people were saying, he would discover at the end that they were often saying nothing. We may talk on a purely social occasion without a specific purpose of informing.

In business, however, we talk because we have a reason for doing so. It is at this stage particularly that we have to raise our language from the instinctive and intuitive level to the rational level. If we talk rationally we talk, in the first instance, because *we want to generate interest in what we say.* We talk in the second instance because *we want to generate understanding of what we say.* Words then become definite. This does mean that we may have to define the senses of our words in certain instances. Thus the spadework of definition becomes necessary to make our meaning clear.

Conditions of Response

Certain conditions must be borne in mind when we talk to people in order to invoke in them a discriminating, or discerning, response—

1. We must know as much of the individual as we possibly can (knowing what a person thinks and feels about his work, and about the instructions given to him, is a matter of great importance).

2. We must have a clear controlling purpose.

3. We must use appropriate language.

Language as a Sign

Technically when A meets B this is described as a dyadic relationship. One may well imagine a situation of two arrows facing one another → ←. A's arrow or communication will depend on B's arrow or response. No two people can meet without transmitting and reacting to signals of some kind. Frequently, undesirable attitudes are created *whilst people are unaware that they are being created.* Of course, once undesirable attitudes are created communication becomes very difficult, if not impossible. Yet we must think of it as part of a situation of inter-stimulation and inter-response that goes on all the time. In fact, two people can rarely meet without either creating a relationship or modifying an existing relationship. An existing relationship is a very flexible thing.

In general, because an organic whole is something more than the mere sum of its parts, any attempt to define and to examine the problem of communication must go further than a sharp division of it (with subsequent separate treatment) into letters, reports, graphic charts, public speaking, instructions and notices. There is evidence enough in every company that these applications call for patient study and improvement: but they cannot be isolated from one another, nor can they be intelligently considered without regard to *coherent general principles*—principles fundamental to all forms of statement or expression intended to achieve an intended result. Training in fluency or clarity is not enough.

Too often, people say that the use of simple English will amount to "talking down" to people. Simple language is not a question of talking down, upwards or sideways. Simple, direct English is the language of information, irrespective of whom one is talking or writing to. Too many notice boards show the kind of turgid, nonsensical "English" typed on perhaps the sixth carbon copy making it all but impossible to read. This is almost incredible, as one assumes that the notice is intended to be read and acted upon.

Personal Aspects

We must refer to the personal aspects of communication. Assume one agrees that the real cause of contented relationships among people, leading to increasing mutual confidence and trust, is effective communication as part of normal operational activity; do we do proper justice to ourselves when we communicate at all? One is helped by the research into this problem by telecommunication engineers. They ask themselves a very intelligent question: "How can we transmit the greatest amount of information in the shortest possible time, at the cheapest possible cost?" (This is a healthy question to ask; and when one does ask it, in practice a great deal of paper work might well disappear.) One result of asking this important question lay in the development of the Morse code. "But," says the telecommunications engineer, "you can never, or very seldom, transmit a message with 100 per cent accuracy." If this is so in communication between machines, how much truer must it be in human communication. There are not only noise, physical discomfort, heat or headache that distort messages; there are the psychological distortions.

In all communication the purpose should be to promote *appropriate attitudes* or action, or purely to promote *understanding* without regard to motivation of any kind. The manner of relating and signifying facts, and the forms of language used to identify and explain them, must be rigorously adapted to the moods and attitudes in which they are received; as they must also be adapted to differences in levels of technical appreciation. The old carpenter, whom William James often quoted, said: "There is at bottom very little difference between men, but what little there is is very important." Even at levels of technological and scientific discourse these attitudes must be taken into account.

Tension

It is impossible for any large group to exist without certain emotional tensions, such as doubts, anxieties, suspicions, jealousies, and even hostilities. These compulsions do distort the transmission and reception of information. For example, if C does not like B for any reason, and B transmits a message to C, C will develop a vested interest in error. He will deliberately set out to misunderstand. In the first place, to understand B would be to pay a compliment C does not intend.

Assume that C is head of a department and B enters it. When B knocks at C's door, C, not seeing B at the moment, says happily, "Come in." B does so, and C immediately recoils. B may be an employee full of ideas and recommendations, and perhaps he gives to C a report containing recommendations for changes in the particular department. C takes this from B, not, perhaps, with a great deal of affection. He knows that if he *accepts* the recommendations it will be tantamount to admitting that his way of doing a thing is wrong, or could be improved upon, and B's way is right. What is C going to do? C would be superhuman if he did not try to find flaws in the argument. He would attack the weakest reasons, and because they are weak he would destroy them and then act as though he had destroyed B's entire case. B, on the other hand, would have been a fool in giving C too many reasons, instead of being logical and giving good and sufficient reasons only. B overstresses his case by giving too many reasons; he gives C the opportunity to attack the weaker reasons and so the distortions are completed.

In human communication, particularly in an organization, it may not be sufficient to be logical. Sometimes it may even be a good or advisable thing to be illogical. It is not sufficient to present people with a new idea, for example, until one first establishes an existing one. The existing idea may be there as a sort of iron curtain—something beyond which the new idea cannot penetrate. By means of consultation and information, one *has* to make some effort to disestablish old prejudices, or old suspicions that no longer have validity. Wilfred Trotter has said that a new idea is the greatest antigen known to science. At least we should clear some ground for its reception.

What is *Language?*

Generally, as we have seen, language does not merely consist in words; it consists in any means by which we convey facts, ideas, attitudes and feelings to other people. The means may or may not be verbal. Facial expression is language, and very often words have a different meaning from the expression accompanying them. As Professor Susan Stebbing has put it in *Thinking to Some Purpose*: "Language ranges from mathematical language at the one extreme of simplicity to gesture language at the other extreme. . . . In speaking to people not merely our words are listened to; the general context of demeanour, manner and tone in which they are uttered affect the degree of attention paid to what we say and, in fact, even the interpretation of our words." In speaking, therefore, the unspoken forms of communication are quite as significant as the verbal forms.

In writing, unwritten forms of utterance are seen in general layout, in spacing, paragraphing, clarity of type and

the like. The unspoken or unwritten forms are often responsible for creating attitudes hostile to or defensive against the
things we say. This, as we shall see, becomes particularly
important at meetings, when the wish is to present a point of
view so that it is understood as intended.

The Meaning of Meaning

We cannot here deal entirely or properly with semantics, nor
will even an attempt be made to do so. "Semantics"
denotes the science of meaning, how words come to possess
significance and how they come to lose it.

Semantics does, however, form one of the grounds of
effective communication. We must at least be sure of the
influences of emotion, context and experience on the various
meanings attached to words. One cannot expect a manager
or supervisor to go through a course on semantics as the
condition of his appointment. But instructions and notices
have to be read and correctly understood. These must never
be ambiguous. It is of the utmost importance, therefore, that
a manager or supervisor should have control of his words,
spoken or written, and that he should be able to distinguish
between *emotive* and *referential* values. Referential values refer
more particularly to meanings in the sense that the meanings
come over as one intends they should.

Although this ability has no priority in thinking about
management or supervision, it is very important indeed.
One can hardly think of individual words without regard to
this ability of evaluation. Words may not be things, but they
can hurt as much as sticks and stones; and they can deceive
wildly. Often a misunderstanding is not real but is simply a
matters of words.

Some words are like a child's pointing finger. They
represent a thing that can be touched or otherwise distinguished. There is little or no problem of definition. There
can be no argument about meanings, for in the last resort the
object referred to can, in fact, be brought in to settle any
argument.

2—(B.648)

Where words are *representative* they can be defined by direct reference to the things represented. As we get away from simple word-labels we may become involved in words that are imagined to mean "something"; but this something cannot be pointed at.

Individual evaluations have been learned by each listener from past experience. The significance of the word will differ as past experience differs. We interpret words in the light of what they seemed to mean to us in the past; we associate them with the meanings that we have learned by this experience. A principal basis of misunderstanding lies in the difference there may be in what has been "learned" from past experience. That a substantial difference in past experience may exist must be realized.

The implications for management and supervision are obvious. A manager or supervisor must attempt to keep communication on a level of definition, where intended values can relate clearly to the outside world of reality.

We can make our communication far more definitive than we do. This is a desirable aim and need not be difficult. It is particularly important where training and instructions are involved.

We can control our thoughts only by controlling language, and we can control language only if we control the senses of our words. In fact the senses of our words and the ways of working with or against one another add up to the rules of reason.

We are afflicted with a terrifying abundance of words, and what fun and games we have with them! We gnaw at them as puppies do at rubber bones. Better control of our language will achieve greater self-confidence, as well as ensuring that people understand what we are talking or writing about.

Although language is a means of communication it is not less often a barrier to it. Abstract words and evaluative terms are obviously ambiguous but, as we have seen, often apparently concrete terms achieve their true significance only in the mind of the person using them.

Operational definition—making one's language clearly refer to the process, things and events with which one is concerned—is a constant responsibility of any instructor. This reference may be best established by the use of visual aids, by demonstration, or by extensive explanation.

So, in viewing language as a means of communication to evoke a discriminating response, we must distinguish clearly between language at the informational or objective level and language at the emotive level.

For our purpose we may use language as a means of communicating with one another; expressing our personal reactions to situations; stimulating a specific response in someone; for the sake of thinking something out. We must make up our minds just what our purpose is and use the language that will achieve it.

If one were cautioning people concerned with the proper use of language, one would say to them: do not use imprecise words as though they have a precise sense; do not use precise words imprecisely; prefer the concrete word to the abstract word; prefer the simple word to the more complex words; avoid colloquialisms and hackneyed expressions which may have lost their original significance.

Language and a True Meaning

What is "appropriate" language? It is language that achieves the purpose for which it is used; inappropriate language is language that does not achieve the purpose for which it is used.

If our purpose is to give information or to clarify a difficulty, then appropriate language as advised by Professor Kapp, Professor Ifor Evans, Sir Ernest Gowers and G. H. Vallins will be direct, simple and definitive or functional. Simplicity does not merely mean the use of one- or two-syllabled words, but also refers to the length of a sentence. The length of the average sentence should not exceed twenty words. Long and short sentences must interchange. In the transmission of written notices, to be read by perhaps thousands of men, the rule of simplicity is not always obvious.

The need for definitive language is obvious enough when we recognize—

1. that the bulk of our vocabulary has no specific meaning; that it derives such meanings as it does have from our individual experience (see page 7);

2. that we are frequently using evaluative terms, the significance of which lies less in any transmission *of sense* than in a declaration of attitude.

A manager may be talking to staff, or on the telephone, or be engaged in an interview, or be talking to committees; he is constantly speaking to people in order to produce a desired result. Thought given to the nature of effective speaking, which we shall deal with in a later chapter, will overcome many of the difficulties that stand in the way of harmonious relationships and will avoid many instances of unnecessary frustration and misunderstanding.

Most people have heard of the near-classical *The Meaning of Meaning* by Ogden and Richards. This book served as a good introduction to semantics, and placed the subject, though not intentionally, well within factory affairs. The book is recommended to those in management and supervision who have to deal with instructions and notices. Also recommended to them, for entertainment as well as profit, are *Language in Thought and Action* by S. I. Hayakawa and *The Tyranny of Words* by Stuart Chase.

Readability

Effective communication between management and workers is, of course, essential to the success of personnel activity. The means of communication vary, but they do include the employee handbooks, house organs, company newspapers and notice boards. These are important, and a good deal of time and money are spent in their production. There is much literature dealing with these media and we shall not discuss here the problems peculiar to each.

That the problem of readability, however, has been neglected is evident. It is hardly touched upon in the books dealing with employee publications. Because readable material in employee publications is essential if it is to have any value at all the problem of readability deserves very careful consideration. Information as to how to achieve readability is rarely given. An editor of a house journal, it is assumed, needs only to be told that his material should be readable, and he will then see to it that it is so.

Nothing is further from the truth. Making a handbook or house organ readable requires as much effort and thought as putting in the journal the right kind of content and expression of view. There can be little improvement on a book written by Rudolf Flesch called *The Art of Plain Talk*. This book should be in the hands of everyone concerned with an employee handbook or house journal. The application of the Flesch formulae will indicate that in any form of communication the material is often written on a difficulty level far beyond the comprehension of the group to whom it is written.

It really is a waste of time, energy and money to publish a handbook or house organ which will not be read with understanding by those for whom it is prepared.

Reading and Listening

The purpose of speaking and writing, as we have said, is to get some discriminating response. The order in which we present our facts, the interpretations we give to them, and the language we use to describe them must be adapted not only to the capacity but to the prevailing attitudes and interests of the reader and the listener. Good explanation is not in itself sufficient; existing ideas must be known and understood.

Spoken communication does not consist in a series of utterances; it is an organic act that depends for reception on the mood it evokes towards the speaker and the utterance.

The words are not merely received and objectively considered; they are received, and their interpretation is determined, in the context of a mood of sympathy or otherwise effected by the speaker's *manner* of utterance.

Context

Context is a vital part of the meaning of a word. We often hear people remark: "Smile when you say that." *Expression* forms an important part of context, apart from past experience. The main point is that when a person uses words in a particular context, he must be careful that the context and the words do not in effect speak contradictory languages. This matter is dealt with more fully in Chapter 11.

We are often concerned with listening to what people say, and what they really intend to convey by their words. This is no easy task, nor is it always enjoyable.

The tendency is to give to words the meanings they have always had for *us*. We do not, as we should, give words meanings they might have for the person speaking. This is yet one more reason for getting to know one's subordinates and colleagues. The more one knows about them, the more likely it is that the meanings of their words will be more evident.

Do not be governed by your first reaction. As a rule people seldom talk to one another, each one is talking *against* what he thinks the other *means*. As a result he confuses what he hears the other say with what he thinks the other means.

People of Varying Backgrounds

Where people of different background and interests try to communicate, misunderstandings can and do result. This happens even when "both sides" are being objective and trying sincerely to get their ideas across effectively.

Always Getting Positive Attitudes

That working conditions should be good admits of no argument, but the procrastinations and delays in making them so cannot be forgiven. Less the subject of agreement are working relations. These can be personally pleasant, but functionally appalling. Persuasion without insight is, like all propagandic influence, short-term and superficial, and *ad hoc* adjustments will in the end destroy and not construct.

Communication and the Importance of Foreign Languages

The importance of foreign languages is a difficult subject to write on, for the reason that in so many ways it is obvious. When in Rome do the Romans, as someone did not say. Obviously, one should improve one's knowledge of languages. To try to argue that we should is to make oneself guilty of a dreary platitude.

Clearly, in view of Great Britain's possible entry into the Common Market, the problem of modern foreign languages is no longer an academic one. We should approach this problem from a more radical point of view than we normally do. We assume that it is polite and convenient to learn a language, that we shall get on more easily if we do. But the reasons for learning a foreign language are far more important, perhaps, than we may conceive.

We know that we can be subjected to real embarrassment when we are in France or Italy or Germany if we do not speak the language. A porter on a Paris station, who obviously could not speak English, tried to speak English when he was getting a seat for an old lady. She looked somewhat disconcerted when he asked her if she would like the engine in her face or whether she would prefer it in her backside. A man was confronted by a Frenchman who likewise was trying to talk English. The Frenchman said, "In case we do not meet again, yes, hallo."

Many people develop a sort of pomposity about languages. There was a magistrate in Ireland who was thus pompous, and he liked impressing people, as many linguists like to do, with his knowledge of Latin. Latin tags being frequently used in court, the magistrate availed himself of every opportunity of using them. He once had before him a really scruffy man who was charged with assault. The magistrate attempted to indicate to counsel who was appearing for the accused that the accused should have been aware of the principle that he should so comport himself as not to injure other people. But, instead of saying this, he said to counsel, "Has your client not heard of the maxim *sic utere tuo ut alienum non laedas*?" Counsel replied, "Oh, yes, he's heard of it. In fact, it's a constant topic of conversation where he works at the top of the mountain."

On the other hand, there are people who speak foreign languages fluently but do not make the best use of them. They do not appreciate the *reasons* for speaking these languages and so do not achieve the kind of personal and sympathetic relationships they should in the countries they visit.

At international conferences there is simultaneous translation which operates magnificently and almost incredibly, but there is yet an appalling loss. Whatever one's ideas are they come over not in one's own voice, not in one's own phrases, not even in the words deliberately selected to emphasize ideas. The real meaning has in fact not come over, in spite of skilful interpretation. A person fails in attending any meeting where one, two or three languages are spoken and he cannot speak them or understand them.

We are generally involved not only in trying to convey understanding to one another, but in creating social relationships with one another; we do not appeal only to understanding, we appeal to *feeling*, and this cannot be done through interpretation in any of its forms. If the work we do extends into foreign territories, then the need to speak a foreign language is imperative if we are to do justice to ourselves.

Unless we create sympathy first we cannot appeal to the understanding. In writing to a Frenchman, a German, an Italian, we must use the words which evoke familiarity, just as when writing to a postman and wanting to describe the colour red, we may refer to a pillar-box. In writing to a foreign person, if we use a word which evokes a familiar reference, we evoke interest. If we use pictorial words, words that illustrate, we are bringing to the fore their understanding of the points we are trying to make.

There is a splendid series of little books which are based on this concept. They are called *The Basis and Essentials* series—*Basis and Essentials* of French, Italian, German, Russian, etc. They deal with those words, and that amount of the mechanics of grammar, necessary to express the most frequently recurring ideas—whether social or in business. They take vocabulary, and first give words that are the same as in English, then words that are similar to English, then words that have a faint resemblance to the English, and lastly words that are utterly different. By application to these little books, a person can build up a substantial vocabulary in two or three weeks.

2 The Manager and Communication

A Chapter on Communication in Industry

THE problem of communication is now at the forefront of the industrial scene. The apparent ineffectiveness of communication in industry has *lately* become one of the most discussed problems of industrial relations: only comparatively *lately*. The problem of communication is not new, but a combination of circumstances has forced immediate recognition of it. Employees are expressing dissatisfaction with the amount or kind of information given to them; management's view of a situation is often not in accord with employees' or unions' views of it; management's statements are subject to challenge. As it has been put: "To give its employees what it feels to be the facts of a case and to maintain in general the favourable opinion of its workers, industry has found it necessary to pay much more attention than previously to *what* is told employees and *how* it is told." Executives now think of organizational effectiveness in terms of human relations and mutual understanding. Good communications in fact support and strengthen any sound organizational system.

Effective communication not only leads to the better presentation of information but is a means of making people more aware of their working environments; it is a means of promoting lasting and good relations. Obedience will then take on a new meaning. People will obey because they *want* to do so and not because they *have* to.

Human Relations

The expression "human relations" is often used, certainly in management courses in industry. What do people really mean by it in the practical, operational sense? How does the term differ from the old-fashioned terms "labour relations," "personnel relations," "staff relations," "employee relations"? One may suppose that the difference in the use of the word "human" suggests the pleasures and satisfactions that people should have in their jobs and in their relations with their fellows.

If a person does not at least have satisfactions in his work and relationships, he will never exert himself to the full extent of his capacity or intelligence. This is not to say that he will not do what he is asked or told to do, but he will not do it well. The sustaining interest born of satisfaction in his work is simply not present. The impetus to do his job well, apart from money, does not exist. But if he has these satisfactions he will exert his capacity or intelligence to the full; he will imaginatively and vigorously deal with his assignments; he will even go beyond them on his own initiative and with his own constructive suggestions. How do we achieve these satisfactions which are conditions for competent performance and willing acceptance?

Before attempting to answer the question let us note that the environment of industry is largely artificial. Nowhere is there a greater conflict of capacities, attitudes, motives and special interests among individuals and groups forced together for a common purpose; and yet nowhere is there a greater need to integrate progressively more numerous and complex items of experience—at the same time developing an increasing *precision* in decisions which can be apprehended and applied. There is not only the need to promote and maintain harmonious relationships in growing organizations, there is also the need to convey more technical information in a way which will enable a more sensitive response to the complex machinery and policies introduced by rapid technological changes.

The general purposes of communication are to produce—

1. greater pleasure and satisfaction on the job and in one's relations with one's fellows;

2. more desirable and more rational attitudes, because of a sense of greater participation and perhaps because of better information about our work environment;

3. a more developed sense of duty, because of clearer definition of authority and responsibility; more intelligent action on the job and perhaps in negotiations.

Information

Effective performance results from the giving and receiving of information; information *given* must be adapted to the kind of information *received*. We may well ask here what kinds of information are intended. The *kinds* of information depend upon the purpose of the information and the company concerned. It would be unsound to attempt to give examples applicable to all companies. Experience gained in different organizations suggests that the common requirements are—

1. information relating to job assignments and the procedures governing them;

2. information which gives a sense of status and participation;

3. information which gives a clearer understanding of authority;

4. information which will enable a better reception of instructions.

We might consider a type of information. Obviously information must be given relating to the kind of job expected of a man. It would be wrong to give him an assignment, about the nature and procedure of which he is not perfectly clear. It is not sufficient, however, to give an adequate understanding of job assignments and the rules and procedures that regulate their practice. Job satisfaction does not arise merely through knowing what the job is or through financial security, but through *security in relationships* with superiors. The better a job is known the more likely a relationship is going to be secure. With that security an employee seeks ways more fully to use his capacities and skills, ways of achieving results through his own initiative and efforts.

The hope is that he will achieve greater competence, greater satisfaction in his work and so be of greater service to the organization. While remaining collaborative, he develops a healthy independence or assertiveness. When understanding is vague, and perhaps dependent on the superior's esteem, one gets a reactive struggle for independence based on fear or dislike—leading to possible friction. Active independence is based on full information or understanding of jobs, policies and motives. Reactive independence is based on suspicion, defensiveness and lack of information.

The Context in which People Operate

In daily activity in industry, whether in the office, on the shop floor or in the laboratory, people operate not only in a context of objective facts and situations, but in a subjective context of attitudes and feelings. Where any communication (including technical communication) takes place, its effectiveness must be measured by the subjective context within which the communication is received; it must also be measured by the context of short- and long-term intentions within which the communication is transmitted. By such considerations we shall reduce the scope of misinterpretation and so of misconception.

The view is still widely held that if people are paid well they are likely to work well. This, of course, is utter nonsense, as few people care to be merely mercenary. Another attempted method of promoting good relations is to adopt the "folksiness" so beloved in America. It is quite ludicrous, particularly in this country, to believe that affability will, in itself, procure good working relations.

Middle Management

Middle management has to apply general policies and instructions to a variety of individuals in a variety of situations. Not only does it have to do this, but it has to report back to top management the results of these applications. It not only transmits information and orders downwards, but it is an important "receiver" for communication up the line.

Apart from the question of whether a middle manager does or does not receive adequate training or encouragement for these tasks, he obviously cannot carry out these tasks properly unless he has adequate information about the ideas and purposes of higher management. The broader his scope of insight, the broader will be his scope of vision; and the broader the scope of vision, the more efficiently will he react to individual situations—and the less there will be of duplication of labour, frustrated or cancelled by the actions of others. The most important thing is that middle management will feel more a part of the organization as a whole, and consequently it will better promote a feeling of organizational membership amongst its own subordinates.

Management by Communication

Communion—or communication—with one's fellows is so much part of life, or should be, that to talk of management by communication is not unreasonable. Good management is individual, and is not a correspondence with a universal nature. If a manager makes communication truly effective, then the task of managing will be easier—never easy, but easier. He will discharge his function with greater skill and accomplishment.

One cannot manage unless there are people to manage. If people respond with more insight, the easier it will be to manage them. If people can be made to think together it will be more likely that they will act together. This does not mean that every order will be accompanied by an explanation of its purpose; effective communication should take place in the normal course of everyday business, creating an awareness of the facts of a person's working environment. Of course facts are not held to exist in their own right, and they are often artificial creations of an arbitrary abstraction. This becomes troublesome when people do not listen to the facts. They listen to what they believe, not to what is said.

There is no intention of becoming philosophical here, however, and what is meant by "facts" is actual happenings or events in a given situation. As it has been put: "The boss-element would shift from the person giving the order to the situation giving rise to it." What people resent is not so much a given order, but the person giving it, with the consequence that the firm may suffer and not know the true reasons for non-compliance.

True Consultation

Joint consultation must regularly take place, not only in the sense of bargaining between management and shop floor, but between a manager and his staff. This will increase competence, and probably willingness, in the discharge of responsibility. As Professor Price of Oxford has said: "If we establish causal necessity, or need, for an action people are more likely to carry it out with greater intelligence."

There is a tendency to condemn consultative committees, rather than to condemn the way they are handled—to condemn a technique because of a failure in its application. Properly-run committees and consultation are the most useful of the forms of communication. In the long run they even avoid paper work and duplication of orders and instructions.

Consultation must be more than a matter of reconciling differences: it must be a matter of achieving *assent* through understanding of the various technical, commercial and human factors involved, and of the various stresses and compulsions that affect them. Joint consultation in this sense will not take up time. On the contrary, if properly run it will take less time than the normal meeting.

As Dr. Wight Bakke of Yale University has said: "Exchange of information and attitude at all levels will achieve many tangible results. It will discourage guesses at or distortion of the facts, or misinformation, with the reluctant misunderstandings that lessen a person's working efficiency; it will provide that understanding of a company and its problems which will decrease grievances due to inadequate information; it will lessen the fears and suspicions an individual may have in his work towards his management; it will facilitate the sense of pride and satisfaction everyone seeks in his work; it will enable people at all levels to express more interest in, and to identify their own interests more thoroughly with those of, the company in which they work."

Communication and Efficiency

It has been suggested that joint consultation has become necessary largely because the normal lines of communication broke down, through the inability of those responsible for maintaining them to communicate effectively; if communications were effective, it is argued, joint consultation might be unnecessary. In fact, as we shall see more fully later, consultation itself, if not wisely handled, may actually interfere with normal communication.

But, in by-passing certain established communication practices, we may in fact set up new frictions and obstacles to effective communication practices.

It is of vital importance to industrial efficiency that far greater attention should be paid to intercommunication within the industrial or commercial unit.

It is essential for the normal lines of communication to be clearly defined and understood. There should be an uninterrupted flow of communication in three directions: downwards from the directors to the operatives, upwards from the operatives to the directors and sideways from department to department at all levels.

The downward flow of communication will be concerned mainly with the interpretation of the policy of the directors, through the various departments, to the operatives who carry out the jobs. The upward flow will ensure that good ideas, grievances and other important questions rising from below get proper consideration when action is taken at the appropriate levels. For instance, a machine operative may have a good idea for improving the efficiency of his machine. He passes the idea to his supervisor, who possibly consults a departmental manager. If the foreman omits to mention the name of the operative who originally put up the idea and tries to take credit for it himself, then communication has failed. The idea may well be adopted, but the wrong man gets the credit; a human relations problem may have been created by the inevitable resentment of the operative.

Similarly, one of the commonest complaints of those on the shop floor is that the directors are ignorant of or indifferent to their grievances. Any actual ignorance and indifference may be the result of either faulty communication from the shop floor upwards or of lack of communication at middle management level.

The benefits to management of good communication are evident if we look at the term "scientific management." For science denotes an appeal to reason as against an appeal to authority or dogma. At all levels people must have the facts to reason on and the opportunity to exercise that reason.

Co-partnership

Government speakers have advocated co-partnership in industry between employees and employers. Whether or not this is immediately practicable or desirable in regard to the economics of industry is somewhat controversial. But certainly co-partnership in the development of ideas, in planning and in effort as between managers and the managed, is both timely and possible.

3—(B.648)

The term "management" should suggest a joint exercise of power, in which subordinates contribute not only effort in obedience to orders, but ideas and points of view which will help to determine the nature and scope of the orders.

That is, all employees—or at least down to a certain level—should participate in the formulation of orders and policies that involve them. Further, subordinates should, in an atmosphere of constructive criticism, be enabled to comment on management practices as they are individually affected by them. This cannot fail to be of benefit to management in its attempts to maintain sympathetic relationships, without which the exercise of authority and the promotion of discipline are thankless and frequently ineffectual tasks.

Conversely, it is equally the right and the obligation of management to appraise frankly the performance of its subordinates. Making entries on merit-rating forms without advising subordinates of what those entries are is cowardly and foolish, and entirely unfair. A man should know his failings and at least be given the opportunity to overcome them. He must know the expected standards of personal conduct and how far he is measuring up to them.

Reaction to Communication

Dr. Bakke has said that communication is a waste of time, effort and money if it falls on deaf ears, or if there is no response to it. When information relating to the company and its operations is shared with employees, it is intended—

1. that the information be received, understood, and believed;

2. that as a result of it people act more intelligently on their jobs and in their negotiations, and develop more rational attitudes;

3. that they understand management better and the compulsions under which management works, as management must understand better the compulsions and uncertainties under which their subordinates work;

4. that they show more interest in, and loyalty to, the company and identify their own interests more thoroughly with those of the company.

These are the primary reactions sought by good communications, which must serve to yield more co-operative and productive relations between those who speak and those who listen. If these reactions are not forthcoming, or not sincerely striven for by management, then the expense (in time, energy and money) of maintaining a consistent communication actively is unjustified. Hence with clear objectives to start off with there must be a constant follow-up and evaluation of communication practices, leading to a weeding out of those practices and procedures that do not get a productive response. There must not be communication for communication's sake. It must be action in order to get action.

A Manager's Objective

Satisfactory job performance is every manager's objective.

To achieve this he has to—
1. convey facts and interpret them;
2. convey attitudes or create them;
3. instruct in skills and possibly improve them;
4. make relations contented.

All this rests on a manager's power to inform and even to persuade. This power must encourage technical efficiency, effective work relations, and understanding of policy. What people cannot understand they fear or ridicule.

The prime factor in good communication lies in a sincere interest and desire on the part of management to communicate as much and as well as possible with employees. Yet three typical views expressed throughout the country are—

1. management gives lip service to communication programmes and often delegates the entire task to staff groups;

2. management's communication is often unrealistic, erratic, synthetic, impersonal;

3. management is unwilling to make the sacrifices of time and energy necessary to communicate effectively, and often depends on expedients.

Some matters for consideration in this connexion are—

1. management and its philosophy about communication;
2. company organization;
3. the means of communicating—the methods and techniques;
4. the conventions or disciplines (both in speaking and writing) that determine whether or not a message is effectively transmitted and received.

Management and its Philosophy

The management factors need little discussion, apart from stressing the need for management to develop a philosophy of communication—to know exactly what it *wants* to convey. Management has failed often to develop a hard, clear-cut philosophy about communication; it does not know its own ideas and objectives in communicating. There can be no depth of conviction about the value of a communication system until management has achieved clarity as to what it is it believes.

There must be a *goal* towards which communication is aimed. Without a clear objective, the effort to *systematize* communications is hopeless. Management must decide what it wants to say, and be sincere and frank in saying it.

Effect of Testing Information

To test the probability that the information shared with employees will be seriously considered, accepted, and lead to a productive response, six practical questions are suggested by a research project conducted by the Labour and Management Centre of Yale University. They are here set out largely as discussed (but with modifications) by Dr. Wight Bakke in an address delivered at Oxford several years ago—

1. Are communications to employees relevant to *their* position and function in the company?

2. Do communications to employees tally with *their* experience?

3. Do the recipients of communications also initiate communications?

4. Are the communications routed so as to strengthen the company society?

5. Do the senders trust and respect the recipients?

6. Can the recipients trust and respect the senders?

"The first difficulty the communicator has to meet is enabling the recipient to interpret and place what is said as having a bearing on *his* position and function. Much that management says has meaning and significance within the special scope of experience and knowledge of management itself, but is meaningless and without significance (if not suspect) to employees. Management must present, along with the information itself, *an indication of its impact on the employees' interests* seen through their eyes and not management's alone.

"Some items of information are so obviously related to the employees' interests, that little specific attention need be given to the difficulty of identification. But what relation do such items as costs, waste, profits, sales, prospects, expansion plans, investments etc. have? What impact on the employee's position and function have such items as company history, products and their uses, expenses and working capital? A man is unlikely to use and respond to information unless he *has* some use for it.

"There may in fact be no possible relevance, in which case the information will not be given. But though the relevance may not be apparent, it may with careful judgement be found to be real; in which case the relevance to the employee's interests must be *established for him*, and judgement of what relevance is, and the expectations it arouses, checked by a follow-up examination of that employee's subsequent reactions. If these reactions disappoint expectations, then the form of the communication must be changed—or the communication must cease.

"A communication is of little value unless an employee is willing and able to understand it and responds constructively to it. This response is only forthcoming if the message tallies with the employee's experience of the activity in the company. To take a further example: a common communication from management to employees is one which attempts to create the conviction that the whole working force is a team with common interests. Merely *telling* them that they are a team is clearly insufficient. It is of little practical use simply to do that, however excellent the communication methods used, unless the actual experience people have with the other kinds of activities that characterize an organization reinforces and supports the message about team work."

In relation to this difficulty, the following sorts of question might well arise—

1. Have *job specifications* been set out clearly showing the way one man is required to relate his work to others? Do functions fail to overlap enough to enable men to experience co-ordination?

2. Is authority autocratic and primarily *directive* in character? Are "upward" suggestions and grievances (especially from line supervision) erratically received? Do they fail to reach top management?

3. Have education and training efforts involved individual rather than group training? Has there been one-way instruction rather than *participating* learning?

4. Are *status* barriers between different levels so rigid that they belie the idea of "team"?

5. Do activities within the organizational structure fail to emphasize the idea of "groupness" and desirable mutual concern for the welfare of everyone?

Other similar questions come to mind; these given are but examples of the types of questions that must be answered before appeals to "team spirit" are issued. *Other kinds of message will demand other kinds of analytical question.*

If any of the above questions are affirmatively answered, the "team spirit" message is not going to be effective. Amongst management, supervisors and workers, all must believe the message: "team-work is wanted, accepted, experienced and rewarded here." People will believe a message if it accords with the activities in which they live; their response then is: "that is true." Exhortations alone are not adequate.

"Many resources of skill and intelligence are lost to a company which doesn't encourage an up-flow as well as a down-flow of communication."

However much men may desire the information shared with them, however actively they may wish to receive and to respond to it, that willingness and activity will fade if they cannot also give information and make constructive suggestions.

There is ample evidence of resistance to information from a management which has not recognized this fact, and has not provided the organizational possibility for this return flow of information and advice from all levels.

Dr. Bakke quoted this report from a shop-floor worker: "We like to hear about management's problems and plans for running their job. But we have ideas too, that come out of *closer contact with the production process* than the management has, and we would like to tell the management about them. If we don't have the opportunity to get these things off our chest we begin to wonder how blind management can be to the facts of life on the factory floor, and how much we can count on the information they feed us. So the worker who does not have the chance to tell management those things is likely to end up by telling management to go to hell. He does that in many ways, but usually in a polite sort of way, by just not listening when the boss talks."

"Communications," said Dr Bakke, "do not live unto themselves alone; they are the nerve system of the organizational body. Their function is not to act independently, but to knit together and strengthen that body.

"It cannot be emphasized too often and too strongly that in this organizational body the foreman performs a key function. He is the agent through whom much of the mutual impact of management on workers, and workers on management, must necessarily be channelled. He is the last link in management's chain of command. He is, in partnership with the union steward, the first link in the workers' demands on, and control of, management; he is their representative authority. He is the focus of management's ability to reward and penalize the workers through appraisal of their work, and of the workers' ability to reward and penalize management by the degree of their productive efforts.

"Frequently . . . top management in its desire to get into direct contact with the workers has short-circuited the foreman and therefore weakened his power to unite the workers and management in other aspects of organizational life . . . *Any communication system which does not strengthen the position of the foreman in that organizational structure is bound to be disappointing in productive results.* For men react not to communications alone, but to the totality of organizational arrangements by which they are surrounded. Communications from top management to workers and from workers to top management which undermine the significance and importance of the foreman by short-circuiting him are taken by workers as admissions by management that their organizational set-up was wrong. For to the average worker the foreman always has been, and is, the company.

"The possibility of making the foreman the primary source of communication of management to workers should not be ignored, or its importance underestimated, by those who are aware that communications are not a panacea, but merely a supporting and strengthening activity for a sound organizational system."

Reprimand

The usual practice in *reprimanding* a person is to be emotional and critical, without referring to what has been done well, as well as concentrating on what has been "inefficiently" done. There must be reference to what has been well done.

Delegation

Delegation must be known and understood. Lord Heywood, when Chairman of Unilever, in a public address to shareholders at an Annual Meeting, mentioned that a matter giving him much concern was that managers did not delegate—or if they did delegate, they did not do it well. A later chapter will be devoted to this problem, but it may be wise to mention now the importance of knowing *how* to delegate as well as facing the *need* to delegate.

Instructions

A chapter will also be devoted to the giving and receiving of instructions and no attempt will be made at the moment to distract attention. Let it now be said, however, that very often an apparent reluctance to carry out instructions is less due to malice than to misunderstanding. Too often a manager asks a subordinate to repeat what he has been told, repetition takes place, and the subordinate then carries out the wrong action. It is quite ludicrous merely to ask people to repeat words, as though words possessed realities of their own and referred overtly to tangible actions.

Initial Objectives in Preparing to Improve Communications

1. Discuss with all management the importance of passing on information to promote sound attitudes and more intelligent operations with less waste or discontent. Emphasize the significance of *explanation* (in terms of facts and reasons), lack

of which often leads to perplexity among middle- and lower-line supervisors.

2. Encourage all management to review their own communication activities and to be willing to improve them.

3. Stimulate the interest of those who are doing well in this field by using their work as example.

4. Discuss simply and in practical form (*a*) the psychological factors involved in our need for fuller communications; (*b*) the several disciplines and conventions involved in our attempts to communicate fully.

5. Review the devices and techniques that have been found most useful in communicating with employees.

Authority and Obedience

Authority and obedience must take on new meanings. Authority should be something assented to rather than something imposed; obedience should be a willingness to do an act, rather than a compulsion to do it. This is especially true when we remind ourselves that the old sanctions behind orders have largely disappeared, and that we cannot make people work or obey rules; we must seek to make them willing to do so. To promote willingness in action, management has the obligation to develop highly efficient communication systems and to appreciate more fully the meaning and significance of effective communication.

Sir Walter Monckton, Q.C., when Minister of Labour, said: "Of the basic elements necessary for the establishment of good human relations I would accept three: the provision of information and the perfection of the art of communication; joint consultation; the recognition of the human factor as of outstanding importance." Recognizing the human factor, and giving expression to that recognition, can be achieved only if management is prepared to make the sacrifices of time and energy necessary to make itself known to employees and to make employees better known to management.

The problem involves not merely getting a free, two-way flow of communication from management to employees and from employees to management, but also the creation of a spirit of team work—devoid of paternalistic attitudes on one side or, on the other side, the prejudices which might grow out of an over-emphasis on difference in status. This stresses "face-to-face" communication throughout the organization —based on recognition of the communication problem as a *social* problem: a problem of the individual in a group society where his way of life, personal experiences, habits, concepts, organization status, all influence his thinking and action.

It means going to the employees; listening to them with an effort to understand their attitudes, what they need, what they want. This implies a two-way exchange of information. It recognizes that the employee's acceptance of a message from management depends largely on the attitudes and prejudices that already exist in his mind.

Production Problems

Management must realize that production problems are related just as much to attitudes as to fundamental skills. The man on the bench can often be as capable of constructive and progressive ideas—given the opportunity, the encouragement and possibly the help to express them—as any more senior person. But he cannot give of his best to his work, nor can he get the best out of it, without enjoying the benefits of consultation on primary matters affecting his activity. Consultation must be between individuals as well as in groups.

Examples of Communication Failure

It may be useful to give a few industrial examples, although why the events should have occurred at all is somewhat baffling:

1. B was once sitting in a senior managers' dining-room of a certain firm. There were about twenty-five managers in the room, four at a table, and everybody was very friendly. B was sitting at a table with a chief engineer and two production men. Another senior manager came in and greeted the chief engineer: "Hello, Harry, how are things?" Harry said: "Splendid, Herbert, nice to see you back again." B said to the chief engineer, "Do you know what he does?" Harry replied, "Don't be ridiculous, I have known him for fifteen years." B said: "This isn't an answer to a very simple question: do you know what he does?" The engineer replied: "Of course I do, he is credit manager." B asked, "What does he do as credit manager?" He received a really brilliant answer: "Well, he looks after credits, I assume." The engineer had no idea of the credit manager's functional relationships, of his compulsions, anxieties, internal and external contacts, of the type of functional problems he encountered. This lack of mutual appreciation was evident throughout the dining-room. It is difficult to believe that after many years there could be this kind of ignorance. Obviously, resentment between departments will occur in inverse proportion to the information obtained.

2. B was in a firm where there were 180 production supervisors. One of these supervisors said: "I do not know how I do my job. I don't know whether I am very good at it, average at it, bad at it, whether I am better or worse than my predecessor. I get my bonus at the end of each year, I have not been sacked; on the other hand, I have not been promoted, so I assume all is well." This gave B an idea, and he prepared a list of some 100 questions which were quite simple: "Does your job require that you *do* so-and-so?" "Does your job require that you *know* so-and-so?" There were three columns into which supervisors were asked to put a tick indicating "yes" or "no" or "I don't know." One hundred and eighty supervisors in a factory of some 4,000 men all differed from one another in their answers on the sheet, in their expectation of what they had to do and to know.

The questionnaire was then given to their managers, and they were asked to fill in the questionnaire as an indication of their expectations of job performance on the part of their foremen. All the managers differed from their foremen and, what was worse, they all differed from one another in their expectations.

3. B was being driven in a company car of a very large organization. The driver started talking about his experiences. The company had had an unofficial strike, and the chauffeur said the convenor came along to transport and asked drivers to join. "We did not," said the chauffeur, "but forty to fifty per cent of us were willing to do so; and I will give you a reason which you may think extraordinary. I have been in this company for some twenty-five years. I have been in transport for probably thirty-five years, but I never get a chance to give my opinion on matters affecting drivers. I am never asked for such an opinion. Often those drivers who have been in the organization for a long time, when on night shift, discuss transport problems, economies and roster systems. The night superintendent comes around and we say, 'We have just been chatting about so-and-so.' But he says he is busy and adds, 'You know the established practice—once a policy and orders are framed you must simply obey them.' The result is that when the strike convenor came round, several chaps said, 'We may at least have an opportunity, if we join, to give our views about things.' "

4. A senior executive once said to B: "You believe that the more information you give to people the more sensitively they react." As this happens with computers there is little reason why it should not happen with people. The senior executive went on: "Does it occur to you that one can go to a great deal of trouble to present people with written information, but they simply do not read what is given them to read?" The visitor asked if he could see the notices and meet some of the men who read them. A group of shop floor workers brought a whole batch of notices to him—works

instructions, shift notices, statements of policy, minutes of meetings, and so on. Although management pointed with pride to tangible evidence of the fact that it attempted to communicate, the notices when they could be read at all, turned out to be written in long-winded and pedantic English. The significant thing is that, in an organization of 14,000 to 16,000 people, spending thousands of pounds a year on communication, nobody appeared to have given thought to the truism that only a very small minority of our community read.

The submission here is not that people cannot read, but simply that they do not make a *habit* of reading. A very obvious point is that if a person looks constantly at a picture newspaper, it is no use writing for him in the language of a superior paper. Obvious though this is, the minutes of meetings in the company concerned, for example, were pompous in the extreme, written in appallingly lengthy sentences and full of pseudo-legal jargon.

The visitor was able to say to some of the secretaries responsible for these minutes: "You use this pseudo-legal jargon because you are mixed in your motives. You use it not because it is the best means possible to transmit information, but because it is most *impressive* to use. Partly you want to give people information, partly you want to establish that you are a good secretary; so you use the jargon of the trade."

One does not wish here to be guilty of distortion by over-simplification. Legal jargon may in certain instances be deemed necessary, but many a time an engineer, a physicist, a chemist, an economist, a lawyer, may address a meeting or write to people. They may be mixed in their motives; partly they may want to give information, partly they may want to establish that they are engineers, physicists, chemists, economists or lawyers; what better way than by using the technical or pseudo-technical language of a particular trade? Many a technical report in industry tells the reader more about the qualifications of the writer than it informs him.

Ten Commandments of Good Communication

(Prepared by the staff of the Executive Communication Course, American Management Association.)

As a manager, your prime responsibility is to get things done through people. However sound your ideas or well-reasoned your decisions, they become effective only as they are transmitted to others and achieve the desired action—or reaction. Communication, therefore, is your most vital management tool. On the job you communicate not only with words but through your apparent attitudes and your actions. For communication encompasses all human behaviour that results in an exchange of meaning. How well you manage depends upon how well you communicate in this broad sense. These ten commandments are designed to help you improve your skills as a manager by improving your skills of communication—with superiors, subordinates, and associates.

1. *Seek to clarify your ideas before communicating.* The more systematically we analyse the problem or idea to be communicated, the clearer it becomes. This is the first step towards effective communication. Many communications fail because of inadequate planning. Good planning must consider the goals and attitudes of those who will receive the communication and those who will be affected by it.

2. *Examine the true purpose of each communication.* Before you communicate, ask yourself what you really want to accomplish with your message—obtain information, initiate action, change another person's attitude? Identify your most important goal and then adapt your language, tone, and total approach to serve that specific objective. Don't try to accomplish too much with each communication. The sharper the focus of your message the greater its chances of success.

3. *Consider the total physical and human setting whenever you communicate.* Meaning and intent are conveyed by more than

words alone. Many other factors influence the over-all impact of a communication, and the manager must be sensitive to the total setting in which he communicates. Consider, for example, your sense of timing—i.e., the circumstances under which you make an announcement or render a decision; the physical setting—whether you communicate in private, for example, or otherwise; the social climate that pervades work relationships within the company or a department and sets the tone of its communications; custom and past practice—the degree to which your communication conforms to, or departs from, the expectations of your audience. Be constantly aware of the total setting in which you communicate. Like all living things, communication must be capable of adapting to its environment.

4. *Consult with others, where appropriate, in planning communications.* Frequently it is desirable or necessary to seek the participation of others in planning a communication or developing the facts on which to base it. Such consultation often helps to lend additional insight and objectivity to your message. Moreover, those who have helped you plan your communication will give it their active support.

5. *Be mindful, while you communicate, of the overtones as well as the basic content of your message.* Your tone of voice, your expression, your apparent receptiveness to the responses of others—all have tremendous impact on those you wish to reach. Frequently overlooked, these subtleties of communication often affect a listener's reaction to a message even more than its basic content. Similarly, your choice of language—particularly your awareness of the fine shades of meaning and emotion in the words you use—predetermines in large part the reactions of your listeners.

6. *Take the opportunity, when it arises, to convey something of help or value to the receiver.* Consideration of the other person's interests and needs—the habit of trying to look at things from his point of view—will frequently point up opportunities to convey something of immediate benefit or long-range value to him. People on the job are most responsive to the

manager whose messages take their own interests into account.

7. *Follow up your communication.* Our best efforts at communication may be wasted, and we may never know whether we have succeeded in expressing our true meaning and intent, if we do not follow up to see how well we have put our message across. This you can do by asking questions, by encouraging the receiver to express his reactions, by follow-up contacts, by subsequent review of performance. Make certain that every important communication has a "feed-back" so that complete understanding and appropriate action result.

8. *Communicate for tomorrow as well as today.* While communications may be aimed primarily at meeting the demands of an immediate situation, they must be planned with the past in mind if they are to maintain consistency in the receiver's view; but, most important of all, they must be consistent with long-range interests and goals. For example, it is not easy to communicate frankly on such matters as poor performance or the shortcomings of a loyal subordinate—but postponing disagreeable communications makes them more difficult in the long run and is actually unfair to your subordinates and your company.

9. *Be sure your actions support your communications.* In the final analysis, the most persuasive kind of communication is not what you say but what you do. When a man's actions or attitudes contradict his words, we tend to discount what he has said. For every manager this means that good supervisory practices—such as clear assignment of responsibility and authority, fair rewards for effort, and sound policy enforcement—serve to communicate more than all the gifts of oratory.

10. Last, but by no means least: *Seek not only to be understood but to understand—be a good listener.* When we start talking we often cease to listen—in that larger sense of being attuned to the other person's unspoken reactions and attitudes. Even more serious is the fact that we are all guilty,

4—(B.648)

at times, of inattentiveness when others are attempting to communicate to us. Listening is one of the most important, most difficult—and most neglected—skills in communication. It demands that we concentrate not only on the explicit meanings another person is expressing, but on the implicit meanings, unspoken words, and undertones that may be far more significant. Thus we must learn to listen with the inner ear if we are to know the inner man.

Communication is not the panacea for all ills. But without it most other disciplines will fail.

3 Logic and Psychology

A Chapter on these Subjects as Essential Conditions of Effective Communication

To devote a chapter to logic and psychology in a book intended for industry may be "starry-eyed" and "academic." There is certainly no intention of submitting that logic and psychology are prerequisites to an appointment as manager. But these subjects are essential to an understanding of effective communication; they deal with necessary conditions to it and must at least be *reviewed*. We have, after all, referred to "semantics" on page 7 under the heading "The Meaning of Meaning" as a science describing another of the essential conditions of effective communication.

This review is not written by a professional psychologist or logician. All technical language will therefore be avoided. In any event, such language would have been left out by choice.

Busy practitioners can skip this chapter without serious loss to themselves.

Psychology

Psychology may be traditionally described as the science of the mind. The subject can be looked at from many different points of view. Differences of opinion among psychologists may in fact be based on failure to appreciate different approaches to the subject. The word "mind" in the course of its long history has taken on many different meanings, and these do not concern psychology as a science. We must, however, try to be exact, and we can look on psychology as "the study of the mind and mental processes as a result of which human beings *think* and *act*." Psychology tries to explain the experiences of an individual as they occur; it tries to understand the various perceptions, memories, imaginings, and so forth, which together make up the mental life. "Consciousness" is the term technically used to describe mental processes as such. "Mind" can be said to be the word that is descriptive of the entire series of conscious states throughout an individual's life.

Enlightenment on our topic of effective communication, and, indeed, for all management practice, lies in the study of experiences and particularly psychological modes of behaviour. "Behaviour" can be studied by observation of another's action or by the observation of one's own conscious states. The word "behaviour" must in practice be used in the widest sense; it must mean everything, from the simplest acts of perception to the complex activities of speech. One can see the relevance of good communication. It must make all essential activities, from perception to speech, easier, simpler, more precise and better informed.

The aim of the science of psychology may be to understand human action; the practical need may be to find out the nature of human capacity, and so perhaps to discover a means of increasing man's efficiency.

In industry it is becoming obvious that the laws of human efficiency are as important as mechanical laws. It is important to know what a man can do, how he can do it and what he needs to know to do it with the best results; to understand this is as significant as to understand production or the laws, for example, for the determination of energy. Greater progress in industry must depend on ever greater understanding of the human being.

The most important study for us is the psychological study of language as the basis for "symbolic" inter-action. In mathematics or the natural sciences, thinking maintains itself against the fantasies and myths embedded in the use of language; they use language which points or refers to things. The mathematicians and the scientists are concerned with external realities, and "inner" reactions have no place in their language. This is not to say that every mathematician or scientist frees himself completely from the presence of fantasy or myth; the difficult task of "excising" may also have to be consciously exercised before pure thinking can be engaged in. The psychological study of language will show inadequate use of language as we know it. It will put us well on our guard when speaking or writing to people.

Logic

If psychology has changed structurally and contextually, and it has, logic may well be said to "take on all comers." The differences between Aristotelean logic and modern logic are as diverse and confusing as can be. When one speaks of "logic," one probably means both formal logic and symbolic logic.

FORMAL LOGIC

Formal logic may be described as the *science* of argument, that is, of inference and proof. People are always arguing; they are drawing conclusions or trying to prove or disprove statements. Arguments are of different types and we shall examine some of them in another part of the book. Formal logic may also be described as the *art* of correct argument. A science may teach us to know, but an art teaches us to do.

A word in formal logic is said to *denote* something when it is normally applied to that thing. A word's *connotations* are the attributes which the word implies. *Extension* is another word for denotation, and *intention* is simply another word for connotation. The more denotations a word has, the less will be its connotations.

The lesson for our use of language is that we should use extensional words and not intentional ones.

With our minds we not only think but feel. "Feeling" includes sensation and emotion. Thinking and *knowing*, however, begin with sensation and *perception*. Logic has nothing to do with feelings, but only describes the intellectual operations of the mind—that is, thinking and knowing. It describes these only in so far as they can be done rightly or wrongly under certain rules. Formal logic may be said to deal with thought as grammar deals with the behaviour of language, or, in other words, with the expression of thought. As language gives expression to both *feeling* and *will* as well as *thought*, grammar can and does deal with interjections and entreaties; logic, which has nothing directly to do with feeling, does not. There is only one formal logic, but as many grammars as there are languages.

When considering the essentials of formal logic, we must observe, as we did elsewhere in the book, that at times it may be inadvisable to be logical. Whilst logic should always reign, there are times when it would be more discreet for it not to take the helm.

The subject is particularly important to us as, like all sciences, it is based on reality, not a fancy or caprice. It has many direct applications for us in the use of language; besides, it gives us practice in thinking clearly about abstract subjects and in developing our own knowledge. Formal logic will help to cure erroneous reasoning. Our conceptions and the language by which we express them are often in themselves indistinct; the rules of formal logic will do something to correct this, too. Our judgements and propositions are also often confused; we do not see when we make a statement exactly what the consequences will be.

SYMBOLIC LOGIC

Symbolic logic is a comparatively new subject. The easiest methods of approach to it have as yet not really been determined. It emphasizes progress from the specific to the general, and its whole treatment of logic is as a science of forms.

The first thing that may strike a student of symbolic logic is that it may have developed along various unrelated lines.

It may be the symbolic expression of traditional or formal logic; it may describe purely the algebra of logic; it may also investigate the laws of thought or logical principles themselves. For a newcomer it is hard at times to see what are the aims of modern logic in itself, and what relations the various branches of it bear to one another.

One would do scant justice to symbolic logic if one tried in the present context to deal with its various applications to language. It may be sufficient merely to say that the applications to language will depend on a full appreciation of the algebra of logic. The most important, from the industrial point of view, is formal logic, particularly regarding the writing of technical reports.

4 Making Inevitable Conflict Constructive

A Chapter on the Effects of Poor Communication on the Nature of Conflict

LET us now examine communication in relation to conflict. Conflict in industry exists, and no amount of effort will avoid it. But consciously constructive effort, involving a personal sacrifice of individual time and energy at each management level, will control its effects and indeed give to conflict itself a character of stimulus and usefulness. Conflict is inevitable and, with increased competition and possible European involvement, will increase rather than decrease in years to come; but if a constructive use of it is possible then, like the holds in judo, its very strength can prove a virtue to those who struggle with it.

There is a difference between a state or condition of opposition and destructive conflict which stems from frustrations that can be avoided. On the philosophical principle of the opposition of contraries, a state of opposition is a necessary condition to the recognition of possibilities and the discovery of *new* creative possibilities.

If organization is to achieve more than an impressive chart on a wall, its formality must have strict regard to the individual personalities involved with departures from orthodoxy and established practice that a regard for individual difference demands.

Organization is a jigsaw not merely of functions but of individuals. These may bring to a function a breath of life that not only animates the function but transforms its character. Often individuals are pinned on the wall in formal place within an organization chart without regard to personality, influence, initiative and the effects that individual qualities could have upon status; the kind and degree of responsibility and authority accorded might result in a loss in both competence and good will.

This might mean submitting policies and practices to the test of criticism—with this difference: the criticism will be informed. In all events a reluctance to submit to criticism, a reluctance to have to support judgement with reason and opinion with facts, is an uneasy admission of doubt or uncertainty in one's own mind.

Or if it is not an admission of doubt, it is an admission of unwillingness to go to the arduous trouble of adducing facts and evidence in support of one's case. Arranging a case, and tactfully presenting it, is an exercise of advocacy that is very taxing, but the effort should surely be made. The threat of arbitrary criticism is lessened when the content of the information we transmit, and the efficiency of the channels of communication we use, serve the purpose of pooling experience and knowledge. This must lead people in departments, and between departments, to participate in the formulation of policies and orders affecting them—at all levels of line management, and it could even be argued beyond these levels to the shop floor.

In post-graduate management courses professional employees frequently express the frustrations of being at the receiving end of orders and policies without having contributed their accumulating knowledge and experience towards the formulation of such orders and policies.

These observations do no more than express a sound principle. As Professor Price has said: "To the extent to which we establish causal necessity for the doing of anything, to that extent do we make the doing of that something certainly more competent and perhaps more willing in execution." The short-term methods of indulgence, persuasion, exhortation, perhaps threat, may be easier and less taxing, but they do build frustrations and misunderstandings. Asserting need and proving it, though difficult, will have long-term effects that will be beneficial, in the interests not only of efficiency but of human relations.

Establishing Need

It seems that this task, well exercised and carried out, is a particular responsibility of management. After all, much management work consists largely in effect in controlling the quality of production not only *post facto*, but in its development.

Supervision needs a particular training in the art of communication; the goal is "understanding," which is not only a condition of satisfactory labour relations, but the condition of the effective functioning of an entire department.

Promoting Communication

Plato has said that he who has the power to set man free has the power to enslave him. Naturally in this modern time one cannot think of enslavement in terms of bodily restriction, but it is possible to enslave a person spiritually, to render competence incompetence, or to reduce alertness to mediocrity. A bad management does these things.

Organization

We must recognize that a group of any kind and any size is not a mere aggregate of individuals such as are enumerated in a census report, but is an association of persons with some degree of give-and-take. The participants may, and usually do, share in some group goal; but they should also get some personal *gratification* out of the joint activity.

Operationally, a group may be viewed as a social unit of interacting persons. It is a *human* association towards which members may have a sense of loyalty, friendliness, co-operativeness and solidarity, expressing deep sentiments of *sympathy* and *identification* with the group name and its aims. It may on the other hand be an association of persons in which is felt a sense of avoidance, dislike, opposition, fear, aggression, and even hatred. Why is this so? The answer, of course, is to be found in the structure, and the behaviour within it, of the group and in the relations among its members.

One must bear in mind here the difference between groups that have intimate, face-to-face association and co-operation, and groups that do not depend in practice on face-to-face contact, and are indeed many subsidiary groups.

Naturally, *structure* will emerge; there must be some kind of order and stability. From the point of view of the members, structure has been defined as a system of differentiated roles and statuses. In addition, structure involves a variety and range of regulations which control roles and make for a certain conformity. This is a matter not only of what we call "division of labour," but of reciprocal *expectations* among the participating members of the group. These roles, and the regulations related to them, serve as principles for the creation, development and maintenance of such social attitudes as exist. Whether or not such attitudes will be constructive or destructive in the inevitable conflict that will exist within a group, will depend upon the nature of such principles or the manner in which they are put into effect.

One can best begin an attempted analysis of conflict with a quotation from Schopenhauer, in his essay *Our Relation to Others*. Indeed, the younger manager will do well to reflect on this essay and the essay by him on *Our Relation to Ourselves*.

Says Schopenhauer: "In making his way through life, a man will find it useful to be ready and able to do two things: to look ahead and to overlook: the one will protect him from loss and injury; the other from disputes and squabbles.

"No one who has to live amongst men should absolutely discard any person who has his due place in the order of nature, even though he is very wicked or contemptible or ridiculous. He must accept him as an unalterable fact—unalterable, because the necessary outcome of an eternal, fundamental principle; and in bad cases he should remember the words of Mephistopheles (in Goethe's *Faust*): *es muss auch solche Kauze geben*—there must be fools and rogues in the world. If he acts otherwise, he will be committing an injustice, and giving a challenge of life and death to the man he discards. No one can alter his own peculiar individuality, his moral character, his intellectual capacity, his temperament or physique; and if we go so far as to condemn a man from every point of view, there will be nothing left him but to engage us in deadly conflict; for we are practically allowing him the right to exist only on condition that he becomes another man—which is impossible; his nature forbids it.

"So if you have to live amongst men, you must allow everyone the right to exist in accordance with the character he has, whatever it turns out to be: and all you should strive to do is to make use of this character in such a way as its kind and nature permit, rather than to hope for any alteration in it, or to condemn it off-hand for what it is. This is the true sense of the maxim—live and let live. That, however, is a task which is difficult in proportion as it is right; and he is a happy man who can once for all avoid having to do with a great many of his fellow creatures.

"The art of putting up with people may be learned by practising patience on inanimate objects, which, in virtue of some mechanical or general physical necessity, oppose a stubborn resistance to our freedom of action—a form of patience which is required every day. The patience thus gained may be applied to our dealings with men, by accustoming ourselves to regard their opposition, wherever we encounter it, as the inevitable outcome of their nature, which sets itself up against us in virtue of the same rigid law of necessity as governs the resistance of inanimate objects. To become indignant at their conduct is as foolish as to be angry with a stone because it rolls into your path. And with many people the wisest thing you can do, is to resolve to make use of those whom you cannot alter.''

This last sentence, apart from being profound in implication, is important when we remember that the structure of industry is characterized by certain power relations among its members. Power has been defined as the effect one person has on another with regard to changing, altering, modifying, facilitating, or inhibiting the other's function, role and status within a given group. Aside from the application of what Schopenhauer said, it is precisely to the degree to which we *facilitate* or *inhibit* function that we make a constructive or destructive use of the conflict that will necessarily ensue.

Developing Ability

Organization should include the responsibility of anybody in an administrative position for developing the capacities of his subordinates—on the principle that a person is not wise in accordance with his length of experience, but in accordance with his capacity to benefit from the experience he is having. As Aldous Huxley put it: "Experience is not what happens to a man, it is what he does with what happens to him." In an organizational situation it is surely a man's responsibility to put certain experiences in the way of his subordinates and to develop their capacity to benefit from the experiences given to them.

Main Sources of Conflict

The main sources of conflict in any organizational structure are as follows—

1. the mechanics of administration;
2. supervision and the methods of transmitting orders, criticism and reprimand;

3. working relationships;
4. working conditions;
5. selection, with unawareness of reciprocal influences.

The stability of any organization is dependent on the information that flows from the organization to its members, and back from the members to the organization.

As has so often been said, people must at least have insights into the situations giving rise to orders, instructions and policy; but beyond this they must appreciate the general motivating forces in their total environment. Whether this is done is one thing; the way in which it is done, assuming it to take place, is another. To establish causal necessity at the best of times is difficult; to establish it at the worst of times requires a rare and practised talent indeed.

Information

Comment is necessary to the passing of information. Opportunity must be given for comment, constructive criticism, and perhaps advice on all matters affecting action. The responsibility of management, if it wishes for the more positive results of conflict, is to develop ways of participation in policy and of action.

Of course, communication systems will vary with the size and organization of the group. In large formalized ones, command and authority work largely by means of fixed and predetermined communication. But it may be necessary to look at these again. Perhaps the skills of those who operate them should be greater than they are. To understand the communication structure of a particular industry we certainly need to know the positions in it. But perhaps the patterns are bad, or the "fixed" communication is wrongly determined; perhaps those who employ them carry out their exercise *by virtue of their function* and not their ability.

The transmission of information, and comment on it, becomes particularly important for professional employees. The scientists and engineers entering industry, after an intensive specialization, are in a sense a new species of intake. They do not in the first place want to be recognized as good industrialists, but as good scientists and engineers. They require all the motivation of any professional employee: a sense of colleagueship, a sense of involvement, and a sense of individual achievement. Many research and development departments would undergo a change if their leaders possessed the ability and the inclination to foster this motivation. Certainly no professional employee will appreciate being only at the receiving end of orders, instructions and policy.

Transmitting Information

How to transmit information to employees effectively is among the most severe difficulties that management has to face. Even at levels of technological and scientific discourse this must be taken into account. A new idea can be asserted, and supported by objective evidence, and yet not be acquiesced in or even acknowledged. People resist a new idea even before they have objectively begun to examine it. This defensiveness against innovation is evident even in the world of pure science where the animosities and practical pressures of industry do not exist. As E. R. Balken of Chicago University puts it: "One has only to review the history of science's reactions to the discoveries of Galileo, Copernicus and Einstein. Cremonius, for example, would not look through Galileo's telescope lest what he might see might be contrary to what he felt he should not see."

Personal attitude and temperament will sometimes delay, if not entirely inhibit, recognition of a submission in the purely scientific world of external realities; how much more easily will there be temperamental "blocks" in industry.

Speaking and Writing

A speaker is not the only active person; his listeners are not merely passive. When we talk to people they are every bit as active as we are; they react not only with understanding and intelligence, but with *feelings*, *emotions*, *prejudices*, *convictions*, *beliefs* and *loyalties*. They are also trying to understand what we say, to associate our message with past experience and to remember what has been said.

The selection of facts and ideas to be presented, and the order in which they are arranged, will be determined by the degree of the listener's intelligence and experience and the *degree to which he is already informed*. To the bare fact of the information will be added any other facts or ideas that the speaker may consider advisable because of the listener's emotional make-up, his knowledge and his beliefs and attitudes.

We have noted that it is a dangerous source of bad communication to believe that words mean what they say, and that others understand them in a particular sense simply because *we* understand them in a particular sense.

Technical Language

Technical language comes nearest to the one-word, one-idea relationship and so is possibly the safest (never entirely safe) language to use. As we shall see in the chapter devoted to reports, technical language may be quite the wrong thing to use. Although it gets nearer to the one-word, one-idea relationship, it cannot be said to do so in all instances.

Obviously a young scientist who has been equipped with a technical terminology does not mean the same things in the use of it as does a person of mature and, perhaps, research experience. Both people are talking the same language but do not mean or possibly even intend the same things. The more a person's experience grows, the greater the particularities he attaches to conceptions.

A writer in a journal, now alas not remembered, said: "Even when the pundit writes ostensibly for the common man, his work is frequently vitiated by the fact that he always has one ear cocked in the direction of Jones-down-the-street, that is, the neighbouring expert in his line, whose withers will be wrung by any departure from polysyllabic precision or by unorthodox analogy, and who is bound, he thinks, to criticize him for levity or ridicule him for inaccuracy. Such a man will never talk, for instance, of 'softening' a piece of steel, because it would not then be quite clear to Jones whether the process referred to was 'annealing' or 'normalizing.' " He will feel compelled to use the technical term whether the non-expert reader understands it or not. "He is so afraid for his reputation as an expert that he dare not, so to speak, take off his coat and be for once a human being."

So the conditions that govern our selection of material, and the manner in which we present it, are in the first place determined by the make-up of the individual to whom the information is addressed. Let us not fall into the danger of addressing our remarks to *types*. We are not speaking to "workers" or "management," but to individuals.

Communication in industry is organization in action. There are times when we can afford the luxury of ignorance and misunderstanding; but when an important part of our job is to translate information into intelligent action and satisfying attitudes, we cannot take enough trouble to say what we intend to say, and so to make a skill of communication.

Quality Depends on Attitudes

It must be remembered that leadership as a power device can succeed in controlling or modifying the attitudes and actions of others only by this recognition; that the quality of an action will depend on the attitude behind it, and that an attitude cannot be created except in terms of the attitudes that exist. Therefore information-sharing and information-*response* will be necessary for the whole administrative and supervisory process if there is to be a lessening of the strains and tensions of the normal conflict that exists.

What training is given to a senior or junior manager in the art of handling his various committees? What training is given in the art of criticism and reprimand? We know that emotional criticism will lead to emotional reaction, for experience teaches this. But what of the express or implied criticism that takes place in conference? Surely there is no greater creator of negative attitudes, which may establish the action least desired.

Handling discussion is an art, not the automatic part of a manager's job. It is a special skill differing from all the other skills and accomplishments that may have justified a man's position. The handling of discussion likely to have serious consequences is not lightly to be given to a man merely by virtue of his place in the hierarchy or his function.

The dissatisfactions expressed about joint consultation are frequently mere expressions of the result of poor chairmanship. Before we can assess its true value, we must see it operate under trained and able men. Indeed no man should be allowed on a joint committee without some training. With it, he can render an incoherent situation coherent; without it, however amiable his personality, or forceful his dogmatism, he will make confusion more confounded.

Knowledge of Organization

Knowledge of a science of organization and administration can never be a substitute for specific experience in a specific organization. But if administration improves its general knowledge of itself and of management theory, it will substitute a rational understanding of behaviour for an "understanding" that is largely based on trial and error and repetitive experience.

Abstract principles of structure may be seen in organizations of great variety; ultimately it may be possible to state principles of general organization; to the extent that administrative organization is aware of these principles, to that extent will it increase its own personal efficiency and lessen the destructive forces of the inevitable conflict within it.

5 Building a Communication System

A Chapter on What Should Precede Establishing a Communication System, with Case Examples

IT is necessary, before establishing a communication system, to examine the actual *needs* of a firm and not merely to imitate the practice of other firms.

So far as it was realistically possible within a short while an attempt was at one time made to discover—

1. sources of any genuine dissatisfaction or discontent within a company, which could be cured;

2. any trends of ill-will or antagonism which were infectious and which might be avoided.

This was done partly by asking specific questions, but mainly through conversation with employees, as conversation is most natural and spontaneous. The picture received, while in certain respects it lacked coherence and detail, did become more complete and better defined as enquiries continued. Association was mainly with senior and junior members of staff.

Finally, the investigator met people "on the floor," in both factory and office. The purpose when talking to any member of the company was dual—

1. to get a frank declaration of attitudes which might reveal what might be needed from both the long-term and short-term points of view to reduce causes of grievance, discontent or lack of harmony, and to improve manager-employee relations;

2. to get people to re-examine the assumptions underlying their attitudes, and so to get them to analyse and extend more fully the situations giving rise to those attitudes.

The General Situation Revealed

The general expressions of opinion seemed to reflect the following points—

1. there was a lack of sufficient inter-managerial communications relating to matters of common interest and concern;

2. there was insufficient inter-departmental communication for full understanding and co-ordination of activity;

3. there was little sense of unity by reason of working in "water-tight" compartments without knowledge of the effects and workings of the organization as a whole;

4. people wanted the opportunity to meet their superiors at regular intervals and for a regular period of time;

5. there was insufficient information reaching the shop floor and the offices to offset rumour and the distortion of facts;

6. there was a general desire for greater contact between members of the Board and junior and senior management;

7. management felt that there was a lack of constant flow of information to them;

8. there was a lack of reaction to recommendations from supervisors, aggravated by minimum positive reaction to demands from shop stewards;

9. there was a sense of a "peace at any price" reaction to shop stewards' demands, enhancing the stature of the stewards and diminishing that of supervisors;

10. there were no proper induction procedures for new employees;

11. committees were not effective; such committees as did exist were not competently run;

12. the foremen asked desperately for adequate status and authority;

13. there were no systematic methods and procedures for training;

14. there were not clear definitions of the range of authority and responsibility that a particular person might have.

Formal means of Communicating

Naturally, information will, or should, exist in the line organization. But apart from information, it was urged that opportunity should be created for meetings at regular intervals. These would provide a means of exchanging views and information among differing functions, departments and sections. These meetings would also enable more discussion of difficulties, problems and work methods.

It was therefore suggested that the meetings might well take the following twelve forms—

1. regularly scheduled meetings of a director, his management and their supervisors;

2. regular meetings between senior management and their shop managers;

3. regular meetings between shop managers and supervisors;

4. meetings between supervisors and employees;

5. the formation of a Works Council. Its representatives should be drawn from management, supervisory staff and employees from the whole organization. From the Council there should be developed sub-committees for safety, the canteen, fire, socials and sport;

6. the formation of a Management Executive Committee, operating as a junior Board;

7. the formation of a Production Committee with representatives drawn from management, supervisors and employees in the factory. The discussion of this committee would range over such subjects as the use of machinery, the upkeep of tools, improvement in production methods, efficient use of productive hours, elimination of defective work, and efficient use of safety equipment;

8. the formation of improved committee mechanisms for negotiations with union representatives. This seemed advisable if one were to avoid the constant confrontation of individual managers by shop stewards. It would probably prove satisfactory to both shop stewards and management;

9. a more intensive use of the company newspaper to communicate essential and helpful information, and so to prevent damaging rumours;

10. a better placing of notice boards coupled with a possible change in that certain notices should be handed to supervisors to place on their boards;

11. preparations of a company notebook setting out company policy, regulations and procedures;

12. preparation of a special supervisors' manual with information that would make him competent to answer questions from his subordinates regarding company provisions and practices.

Informal Means of Communicating

In addition to committees and line communication, employees and members of management sometimes sought the opportunity for the discussion of individual case problems. There was the desire to "talk something out."

A suggestion was made for immediate courses on—

1. appreciation of the problems and convention of communication; and

2. the proper handling of committees.

The investigator felt that there should be no question of "sides" in an industrial committee, but only differences in responsibility, though different views of responsibility may be directed to the same purpose. The committee leader should establish a basis of honest purpose.

Experience with Middle Management

We have already said on another page that it matters less what you do than the way you do it. Top management in a firm of size were complaining about the lethargy of their middle management, and they said also that they simply had no contact with them. A meeting *of middle management* was organized for them. Supervisors and shop managers came to the meeting, which was being conducted for the Managing Director. At the meeting discussion was entirely uninhibited, both supervisors and managers complaining of lack of information about important jobs. This was reported to the Managing Director, and he said that he would hold a similar meeting. He did so, but could not get the participants to speak. The person who had first conducted the meeting did so again, with the Managing Director present, and once more all spoke freely.

Shop Stewards versus Foremen

The foremen of a firm were very bitter about the allegation that when they had altercation with stewards, senior managers on every occasion took the part of the stewards; they feared a strike or "go slow" if they upset the stewards. The company in question prided itself on its good industrial relations. Seldom could people engage so naïvely in self-deception.

The senior managers at the time were nevertheless holding meetings to discuss improvements in discipline. They were told of the complaint by the foremen, and they then bore this very much in mind when deciding the issue before them. What is so puzzling is that while the foremen brooded under this discontent their managers were unaware of their feelings.

6 Pooling Experience in Deliberation

A Chapter on Meetings

COMMITTEES and discussion groups, or conferences as the Americans call them, are not popular at the present time. Their failure effectively to achieve the results they intend is largely a failure in chairmanship. Within any type of organization, industrial or otherwise, the chairman is normally selected because of his role or status and not because of his ability. If meetings are to have value, and they are after all one of the most important of the forms of communication, then chairmen on whose handling of meetings might depend production, training, welfare or financial affairs, for example, must be trained. By training is not meant necessarily that they must submit themselves to some external tuition; what is certainly meant as a minimum is that they should train themselves by evaluating their experience competently. To cite length of experience as a necessary qualification for leadership at a meeting is quite irrelevant. In order to evaluate experience adequately a person must ask himself appropriate testing questions.

It is not sufficient nor adequate to run meetings according to formal procedures. These can be known through a reading of a multitude of books and require no special aptitudes. The Law speaks of a "reasonable man," does not believe there is such a person, and issues all sorts of *caveats* and requires compliance with formal "gimmickry" including the absurdity of the vote. The vote encourages lobbying or pressure groups. Formal proceedings as such have little or no application to industrial meetings less than twenty. For the application of formal procedures, if the chairman and his members are to be adult, he must substitute logical procedures.

The talk of average persons as being "reasonable" is nonsensical, as it requires rigorous discipline to apply the laws of reason before arriving at a judgement. If the chairman does not possess this ability to maintain reason, it is a fairly safe bet that the meeting will not care to help him. Perhaps this is the function of the unfortunate secretary.

The fact that the chairman has to get people, who normally think and talk casually, to think and talk rationally, in order to arrive at rational judgements, is a duty which he must discharge. If the chairman is unwilling to do the hard work expected of him then he must decline to be a chairman, in spite of his role or his status. A chairman cannot assemble and evaluate facts, establish interpretation of them and inferences from them, formulate problems and name the factors relevant to their solution, and so on, by striking the table with what is politely called a gavel (which is nothing but a hammer), or otherwise beating a tattoo in front of him.

Meetings, or conferences, are associated with reflective thinking. This is said with due knowledge of the value of "brain storming" sessions, "group dynamics" as it is called at Bethel, and the general emotion and drama potentially present whenever people discuss matters of common concern and interest. Because meetings *are* associated with reflective thinking the very essence of them lies in the question and answer. The chairman therefore must at least develop the art of asking questions and insist on precise answers; he should not put pseudo-questions or engage in quite meaningless utterances such as: "What do you think?" or "We have not heard from you for some time, perhaps you would like to say something."

If full discussion at any meeting is desirable, a chairman must do more than follow formal procedures; he must stimulate sound thinking and careful judgements. If a meeting is to have the benefit of a member's views, assessed in the light of his experience and special knowledge, the chairman must promote rational discussion in an atmosphere of mutual confidence. Only in this way will it be possible to encourage an acceptance of new ideas and improved practices.

Meetings in Industry

No business or industrial organization can get along without a large number of meetings. Meetings, when properly run, are probably the most valuable of a company's means of communication. They are certainly necessary if we are to promote—

1. understanding and willing acceptance of policies and procedures;

2. understanding and tolerance of people's needs and desires; "two-way" exchange of constructive suggestions and ideas; intelligent co-operation;

3. saving of time, repetition and paperwork.

If meetings are to help to achieve these ideal ends, they cannot be run merely according to formal committee rules. The chairman cannot simply be a man in the chair who is there to keep the meeting to order and to apply rules of procedure.

Meetings within a company are of so many kinds that it may be necessary to make some distinctions clear. We shall constantly stress, however, that all meetings are forms of communication. At all of them there must be some effort to promote or improve personal understanding.

Meetings vary between the following two extremes—

1. highly formal—chairman, secretary, average agenda, usual minutes, formal rules of procedure;

2. very informal—*ad hoc* meetings about current business: these may be meetings of close colleagues, perhaps on first-name terms.

In day-to-day working of an organization, meetings of type (1) are probably the exception rather than the rule. Therefore we shall usually from now on speak of the person chairing a meeting as the "leader," rather than as "chairman." The word "chairman" implies a degree of formality that is inappropriate and unhelpful in the majority of meetings.

In addition to having degrees of formality, meetings vary in nature in many other ways. For example the main objective of the leader, throughout a whole meeting or at different phases of a single meeting, may be—

1. to give information;
2. to get information;
3. to solve a problem;
4. to secure certain positive attitudes.

At any point in the conduct of a meeting the leader must know which of these four objectives is applicable.

Causes of Unsuccessful Meetings

Let us consider briefly some of the causes of ineffective, frustrating or boring meetings—

PREPARATION

Inadequate advance information, faulty composition of group, leader vague about subject or purpose, lack of provisional plan, bad handling of time-factor, physical conditions inadequate.

INTRODUCTION

Too long-winded, incomplete, too short, muddled or confusing, key terms not defined, main issues not clarified.

LEADER'S ATTITUDE

Too autocratic, too dogmatic, too easy-going, bored and uninterested, insincere, inattentive, over-serious or pompous, too flippant, intolerant or tactless, partial to particular members, prejudiced.

CONTROL AND GUIDANCE

Irrelevant rambling, latitude to over-talkative, diffident members ignored, discouraged or snubbed, fruitless argument, private discussions, random allocation of time to major and minor issues, subject too big or too thin for time allowed, contributions ignored, disagreements or misunderstandings not clarified, tempo too slow or too fast, intermediate phases of progress not summarized.

CONCLUSIONS

Not summarized, minority views ignored, inaccurate quotation of contributions, unsettled points left "in the air", action required not formulated.

Participation

We have considered the causes of unsuccessful meetings. Many of these arise because the leader did not develop a "sense of participation" in the members of the group. This sense of participation is not only a matter of the amount of talking done by members of the group or by the group as a whole. It is largely the result of the attitude of mind with which the leader comes to the meeting.

Not all meetings are expected to arrive at decisions or to make recommendations. Therefore the amount of participation wanted will depend on the type of meetings. One can range from no group participation at all (which is rare) to the fullest possible participation. By "full participation" is meant: all members of a meeting contributing from their experience and knowledge to the achievement of the meeting's purpose. By "limited participation" is meant: members at a meeting, though not expected to enter into full discussion, yet being encouraged to ask questions and to express views so as to make as full a contribution as possible to improve general understanding and to achieve the meeting's purpose.

Can one believe that any meeting—whatever its nature—can afford to avoid questions, voluntary information, or critical comment?

Types of Meetings

Some meetings do not aim at full discussion or participation. Members are primarily expected merely to listen to what is being told to them.

Examples of meetings where full participation is not expected—

1. meeting called to hear a statement of policy;
2. meeting called to hear definition of responsibilities;
3. meeting called to receive instructions;
4. meeting called to receive explanation of new system or procedure.

Even at these kinds of meetings should there not be some opportunity for those affected by policies and instructions to discuss them briefly—to express views based on their experience in carrying out policies and instructions? Developing our own ideas and plans may be quite praiseworthy, but sometimes we need criticism of them and timely correction of them.

Apart from receiving information, is the meeting not called to promote willing and keen co-operative action based on the information? We must be able to assess in advance the degree of support that a policy or action is likely to receive. In all events the person convening and addressing the meeting *must make his meanings clear and ensure understanding*.

Other meetings may require group participation, and yet not be intended to arrive at decisions or to make recommendations. For instance, meetings called solely to exchange information or experience.

The executive may make the final decision, if any is necessary, or each individual may make his own decision in the light of the discussion. But even here, when there is no effort to reach a group decision, discussion must be purposeful and relevant.

The leader must know how to guide the discussion so that it does progress and remain relevant—does lead to understanding of one another's difficulties and viewpoints.

Another type of meeting is one called merely to air attitudes and feelings, to "let off steam," to ventilate complaints and grievances. Here, again, it should be possible for individual members at the meeting to receive some benefit and stimulus from listening to other points of view and other experiences. Through judicious questioning, the opportunity exists not only to have a safety-valve, but to get people to re-examine their attitudes and beliefs and the assumptions underlying them.

Some meetings are for the purpose of co-ordinating different organization levels, or for co-ordination on a particular level. At these meetings of people with different functions and responsibilities, we should again exchange experiences, and so know more about one another's functional difficulties.

In all these four types of meetings it is clear that the chairman or leader has a most important part to play.

The problem-solving meeting is possibly the most important. This type of meeting may be described as one where we try to transform a situation in which we experience doubt, conflict, or a disturbance of some sort, into a situation that is clear and coherent. We may try to reach a solution of some kind, e.g. the formulation of a policy or the solution to some technical or administrative difficulty, and decide on or recommend a course of action; or the conclusion we try to reach may be a satisfactory description of the *meaning* of a situation as agreed to by the committee—that is, the problem may be to clear up confusing and contradictory interpretations of terms or facts.

A common example of a problem-solving meeting is the "post-mortem" meeting. Because something has gone wrong or some mistake has been made, the meeting is called to find out precisely: what went wrong; where it went wrong; why it went wrong; how it can be prevented from happening again. Here, the leader must—

1. give and get information about the situation which has arisen;

2. stimulate a combined effort to solve the problem of preventing a recurrence;

3. encourage constructive attitudes and opinions to gain effective co-operation in making the adopted solution effective.

When a committee is called together to solve a problem, it is because we are of the opinion that there should be an association of minds in thinking and acting; because we consider that group judgements may be superior to the judgements of an individual. Most problems need to be examined from the points of view of all concerned—not simply from the point of view of one person.

In this sort of activity we became aware of facts we did not know about, and our ideas and attitudes are modified or strengthened by the contributions of others. We are engaged in learning. In the statement and discussion of problems we might bear in mind the interrogatives What? How? When? Why? Who? Where?

At all these meetings, if there is to be any intelligent talking we must—

1. know exactly what we are talking about;
2. keep our talk relevant;
3. know exactly where there is disagreement, and why;
4. know exactly where there is agreement.

Reflective Thinking

In all five types of meetings our activity—encouraged and inspired by the leader—should be a thinking activity, and not a random or emotional one. Thinking means that we want to know as much as we can about the causes and results of events and policies; we want to know about the advantages of proposed courses of action; we want to know the reasons for people's views; and we want to know the significance and the results of our own views and actions.

That is, reflective thinking involves consideration of evidence. We are concerned with experience, meanings, causes, results, advantages, disadvantages. We want to come away from a meeting knowing more, and understanding more, than we did before the meeting.

We most often think and speak in a rambling sort of way. But if we are interested in the particular outcome of our thinking and speaking, we cannot allow these activities to be casual and undirected. Sometimes we need not worry about an incorrect belief. Mistaken ideas or prejudices do not really matter if they do not involve us or other people in difficulties or in trouble. But when, as in industry, there is practical pressure, when we find ourselves caught up in an urgent problem on the solution of which the effectiveness of the organization depends, there can be no doubt about the need to think well, and to test the truth of what we believe. We cannot afford indulgence in our prejudices or in hasty judgements. We must arrive at sound solutions. Incorrect notions may have very unfortunate results.

When we are trying—

1. to explain something or the need for some action;
2. to give information;
3. to modify unjustifiable attitudes, and strengthen constructive attitudes;
4. to solve a problem;
5. to find out the meaning of a perplexing situation;
6. generally to reach a conclusion which is trustworthy,

then thought must become reflective; that is, it must be deliberate and questioning.

The leader is primarily responsible for seeing that members at the meeting behave in a constructive and thoughtful way. Can a leader be said to have discharged his important function simply by exercising rules of procedure?

Discussion is more than a matter of free talk or conversation. Casual conversation may promote good fellowship, but it does not enable us to understand situations or to solve problems. Discussion is both thinking and talking, not merely talking. And the talking is intended to aid the thinking. Good discussion—

1. stresses reflective thinking rather than emotional activity;
2. aims to understand a situation or difficulty;
3. aims to appreciate meaning and significance;
4. aims to analyse and solve a problem;
5. occurs in a group situation.

What counts is what the committee as a whole thinks or feels, and not only what some able or forceful individual thinks. Discussion is not a debate. In a debate a person has made up his mind about something, and wishes to convince everyone else that he is right. We attend discussion meetings to learn, in order that we may be in a position to make up our minds.

Functions of a Chairman

A discussion leader must know—

1. how to plan and prepare for a meeting;
2. how to start a meeting;
3. how to stimulate and guide discussion;
4. how to get everyone to take part;
5. how to prevent irrelevancies;
6. how and when to give intermediate summaries;
7. how to bring a meeting to a conclusion, and to give a final summary so that everyone knows exactly what the meeting accomplished;

6—(B.648)

8. the kinds of actions that delay, handicap or wreck a meeting.

The use of method will get thoughtful and constructive participation where it is expected, and move to decisions that will lead to co-operation in action because there has been co-operation in thought.

We are not concerned with putting matters to the vote. If a meeting ends in a vote it may indicate that the meeting has failed. People who vote on a matter have often given no thought to it. They vote because of a prejudiced belief, or because they want to conform. Interest is in weighing judgements, not in counting hands. To encourage the practice of voting is to encourage pressure groups or lobbying.

Leading a Discussion

The five steps for leading a discussion are—

1. OUTLINE SUBJECT CLEARLY

State topic, problem or difficulty with which meeting is to deal; outline situation giving rise to topic, problem or difficulty; state purpose of the meeting, so that everyone knows what is appropriate for discussion and what is not appropriate; define technical terms used; outline the procedure to be followed. (Suggest a logical "pathway" for the discussion.)

The vague statement of a subject is the cause of most futile discussion. The subject must be simply and clearly expressed, and all ambiguous words must be defined. If possible the subject before the meeting should be put as an impartial question. The subject must be worded in such a way that discussion will be limited. Some subjects at meetings are so broadly stated that it is difficult to know just what the field of enquiry is. One advantage in stating a subject in the form of a question is that a question provides the framework for the answer.

The situation giving rise to the subject must be explained. A meeting wants to know: What is the situation? What is the state of affairs needing change or improvement? In all events, to get discussion started, it is best to introduce some specific topic or illustration arising out of the general matter for discussion.

2. GUIDE THE DISCUSSION

Assemble all necessary facts; draw out information, viewpoints, experiences; make sure that all contributions are understood; keep discussion on subject; avoid purely personal arguments; develop group participation.

The leader must make sure that all available information is before the meeting, and he must get such further information from members as is necessary. He must stimulate thinking and get the meeting to examine the experience and judgement of all.

When we speak of members accepting the final conclusions of the meeting we should mean that, through enlisting the thinking and participation of all, the leader gets members to accept a conclusion which they produced.

All members differing from one another in degree of knowledge and experience must be drawn into the discussion. Questions must be particularly directed to those lacking conviction.

3. CRYSTALLIZE THE DISCUSSION

Summarize the development of the discussion; refer to any changes of opinion; state points of agreement and disagreement; state intermediate conclusions as reached; make sure of understanding and acceptance of summaries.

When discussion has gone on for some time it is often difficult to remember all that has been said, and just where agreement or disagreement exists. The leader must give a focal point to the discussion by giving short summaries from time to time. A particularly good time to give a summary is when the leader notices that uniform thinking has been reached on one phase of the subject, and no really new contribution is coming forward.

There should, of course, be a summary when each intermediate conclusion is reached. Summaries are also useful to bring discussion back to the point and purpose of the meeting when the subject has been extended beyond profitable limits.

4. ESTABLISH FINAL CONCLUSIONS REACHED

Give final summary of course of discussion; state conclusion clearly; state the main points contributed at the meeting; state minor disagreement (if any) and the reasons for it; check to be sure of a fair summary, and that members understand it.

A final summary is necessary, before the meeting ends, to make clear exactly what the meeting has accomplished. Restate the subject in the form of the question originally put to the meeting. State the main points of the discussion leading to the intermediate conclusions, and so to the final conclusion. Ask members whether the summing up has been fair and complete, and invite any comments.

5. GET AGREEMENT ON ACTION (where the meeting warrants it)

Show that the decision is a group decision arising out of discussion; show that decision is based on conviction, assent or reconciliation of views; formulate the action.

The action to be taken must be fully understood. Whether the purpose of the meeting be to decide on action, to recommend action, or to get acceptance for action previously determined, it is the leader's responsibility to summarize the reasons for it and show how it is in the company's interest. Where there has been full discussion, it will be easier to get acceptance for action. The suggested action will then be the result of the group's judgement. Group judgements will always lead to more responsible actions, since people will do what they have decided—not what they are required to do by a majority decision.

How to Get Ready to Lead a Discussion Meeting

1. DETERMINE PURPOSE OF MEETING—

   know the objective, e.g.,
   to develop support for required action;
   to consider unsolved problems; to understand a situation;
   to settle disagreements.

2. EXAMINE THE SUBJECT—

   get facts and information on the subject; determine points that need discussion; anticipate possible differences in viewpoint.

3. ANTICIPATE CAUSES OF DELAY AND OBSTRUCTION—

   prepare for the difficult member and for embarrassing subjects.

4. OUTLINE THE DISCUSSION—

   know final objective;
   know intermediate objectives;
   frame appropriate questions;
   outline clear introduction;
   quote case-examples;
   prepare a time-table.

5. HAVE EVERYTHING READY—

   help members prepare, e.g. agenda, reading matter;
   issue announcements in good time; arrange accommodation; prepare visual aids and other necessary material.

   Preparation for any meeting is essential. An ill-prepared meeting will most often lead to vague and wasted talk. It is first necessary to know the object of the meeting—the purpose for which it is being called. Meetings often continue for some time in a state of confusion. Participants do not know just what is expected of them.

A meeting may fail to come to a decision on the problem under discussion and may yet have been a valuable meeting. It may come to a perfectly logical conclusion that now is not the appropriate time to decide; that the committee is not ready to decide; possibly that other persons should be called in to participate in the decision; or that the meeting be adjourned for further information. A decision not to make any decision at this stage may be the best action for the committee to take. But the absence of a suitable decision may be due to the leader's inability to conduct the meeting adequately.

In a meeting intended to arrive at a decision or recommendation, the leader may be convinced in his own mind what that decision or recommendation should be and seek to influence it. This is in order, provided he allows full and free discussion by members, and is open to the realization that he may be wrong. By encouraging analysis of the situation and assembling facts in support of his view, he may promote understanding which will lead to agreement with him. He must strive to attain that objective.

It may be said that these activities are engaged in at every one of most meetings. But at any given moment a good chairman can only be doing *one* of these things. Very often, for example, a meeting becomes emotive, and one encounters all the humiliation and degradation of a chairman thumping the table, calling for order and making a pious plea with members to speak "through the Chair." This is, of course, a dismal confession of failure. The point is that a good chairman should say to the meeting: "I have called you together to answer a question. You are not doing so, but declaring your attitudes to the question. Maybe the question is wrong and should be differently formulated. If it is correct, let us now devote ourselves to our attitudes to it, and with the attitudes known I shall call you back to answer the question." One cannot make an angry man think. It is no use saying he should think, or is paid to think: he simply cannot think. A sullen man *won't* think. Again, it is no use making ethical predications, he won't think any more than a man with toothache will think. The latter's entire field of consciousness is centred in his tooth. Table rapping will not make amends.

Establish points of disagreement and the reasons for it. Disagreement is not dangerous but, as the very basis of dialectic, is inevitable. What is dangerous is failure to know the reasons for disagreement. I am quite prepared to assent to something with which I disagree, provided I have been given an opportunity to state my reasons for disagreement.

The chairman must establish agreements and why they exist. Once again, agreement *per se* has little meaning. What is important are the reasons for agreement, and these must be known to all members present.

The chairman must establish relevance. If he is to do this properly, he must have a yardstick by which relevance can be measured. It is not merely a matter of opinion whether it exists or not.

The chairman has to *prepare* for a meeting. By preparation is not meant merely collating documentary information for the meeting. Much more is involved. Preparation does include preparation of a verbal map. In other words, there must be time to think. If, as one is often told, there is no time to think owing to pressures, then the whole matter admits of no further argument.

The preparation sheet and the expository preparation sheet on the following pages show the form a discussion might profitably take.

PREPARATION SHEET

(*a*) The question is ....

(*b*) What are the chief facts or events that lead to the question? ....

(*c*) What are the chief causes of these disturbing facts or events? ....

(*d*) What will be results of these causes if nothing is done about them? ....

(*e*) What goals or aims should be kept in mind in considering the question? ....

(*f*) What explanations are advisable?

What is meant by? ....

What is meant by? ....

(*g*) What are possible solutions? ....

What are the advantages? ....

What are the disadvantages? ....

(*h*) What solution is on the whole preferable? ....

What are the advantages that make this solution preferable? ....

What are the practical grounds that justify this solution? ....

(*i*) What is the programme for putting solution into effect? ....

EXPOSITORY PREPARATION SHEET (*for example, in the statement of policy.*)

(*a*) The question is ....

(*b*) The question is of importance in that ....

(*c*) Causes giving rise to the question are ....

(*d*) Results if we do nothing about the causes are ....

(*e*) The terms to be defined are—

By .... is meant ....

By .... is meant ....

(*f*) Proposals for the dealing with this question are—

(1) .... (2) .... (3) ....

The advantages of (1) are ....

The disadvantages of (1) are ....

The advantages of (2) are ....

The disadvantages of (2) are ....

(*g*) This solution is on the whole preferable—

....

The reasons why it is to be preferred are—

....

(*h*) The programme can be put into effect in the following way—........................

Leader's Authority

Although a leader must guide, he must also exercise control and discipline. But he can do this without relying on his weight of authority and on formal rules of order. We don't want formal procedures. We want collective thinking.

Introductory Remarks

A great deal can be said in little time when all irrelevancies are avoided and a logical pattern is followed. The following information can, and should, appear in the introduction—

1. a presentation of the subject. The leader must emphasize its importance and inspire the meeting to want to deal with it;

2. an outline of the situation giving rise to the subject, with some specific case to illustrate the situation;

3. a definition of technical terms likely to occur.

Questions

Now let us consider the art of asking questions. Questions can be used by the leader not only to ensure that everybody does take part at a meeting, and to make the best use of each member's knowledge and experience, but also to open up discussion; to amplify and explain each member's contribution; to introduce a point which is being overlooked; to move discussion ahead from one point to another; to bring out the distinctions and similarities between the various ideas; to encourage intelligent judgement on the ideas presented; and—not the least important—to exercise discipline.

If the leader makes use of a questioning technique, he will find it far superior to the chairman's gavel in promoting co-operation and team work.

INFORMATIONAL QUESTIONS

These questions are fact-finding—they are used to get some specific information. They are necessary to establish a sound factual basis for discussion, e.g., How many and how much? In what month? What is the price? Has your department experienced these difficulties? What has caused this situation?

EXPLORATORY QUESTIONS

These valuable questions are not used as often as they should be. They usually fall into the how and why category. Not all questions that begin with these words are exploratory. "How long have you worked in the department?" is an informational question. "How can we reconcile these facts?" is an exploratory question. Exploratory questions mainly probe into the reasons for people's views.

When reasons are brought forth, they encourage the wider thinking of the committee. The questions also sound the degree of conviction with which an opinion is held. Where a person is honestly convinced about something, he will not hesitate to give the grounds for his belief. Where the belief is a "convenient" one to hold, or is merely prejudiced or stubborn, the exploratory question will soon reveal that the particular member cannot justify his belief or attitude.

The exploratory question will also bring before the meeting the degree and quality of a person's experience in support of his contribution. Generally we may say that the exploratory question enables us to assess the value of a member's contribution, secures a clearer statement of the meaning and significance of a reply, encourages the thinking of the committee.

OPINION QUESTIONS

These questions are used to get a ready expression of opinion from a member—more particularly from the member who is not volunteering his contribution.

QUESTIONS TO CLARIFY MEANING

Often a member's contribution is vague, or he expresses himself badly, or he uses unnecessary jargon or technical language. The clarifying question becomes necessary, e.g., "Could you please restate briefly what you have just said?" or, "If I understood you correctly, I think you meant . . .?" These questions are also useful to interrupt the "long-winded" speaker.

EVALUATING QUESTIONS

These questions develop the possibilities of a particular contribution, or of some important aspect of the discussion, e.g., "What would be the good (bad) results of the suggestion just made?" or, "Which of the suggestions just submitted would get the quickest and best results?"

Ways of Asking Questions

When we speak of guiding discussion we are aware that no two members of a committee are alike, nor will they respond to exactly the same kind of treatment. Some members with wide experiences are reluctant to talk about them. Others, with limited experience and limited knowledge, may tend to talk too much. Some members will not be as interested as others. An effort must be made to stimulate their interest. Others will be so interested that they may tend to dominate.

We cope with different forms of behaviour at a meeting, and generally set the pace of the meeting, by varying the use we make of our questions.

There are two main ways of asking questions, whether they be informational, exploratory or any other type.

1. *Overall questions* are put to the group as a whole. They are put generally without naming a specific individual.

2. A *direct question* is put to a particular individual.

The question may start as one put to the whole committee and then, if there is no answer to it when put generally, it may be directed to an individual.

The most important thing about the direct question is that it is addressed to an individual best qualified to answer it. There is no point in making a question a general one when a member with appropriate knowledge and experience is best equipped to answer it first—thus saving a lot of wasted and desultory discussion.

The direct question has a number of valuable secondary uses.

It can be used—

1. to "bring back" people who have mentally "left" the group;
2. to draw in the silent member;
3. to break up side discussions. There is no need to use the gavel. A direct question addressed to one of the members engaged in a side-discussion will stop it;
4. to get away tactfully from the too-talkative member;
5. to get confirming or opposing views;
6. to throw back to some member questions directed to the chairman.

Too many direct questions can have a bad effect on the spontaneity of the group. Members will not volunteer answers. They may feel that they should not speak unless addressed. Consequently, direct questions should be alternated with general questions, to keep the whole group active and alert.

The main uses of the overall question are—

1. to get immediately two or three volunteer expressions of opinion—revealing knowledge and experience which the leader did not know the members possessed. He will soon realize whom he can count on for valuable contributions. Having got two or three expressions of opinion through the general question, the leader can by direct questioning get individual members to evaluate the opinion;

2. to throw back to the whole group questions addressed to the chair;

3. to discover any general change in thought.

The leader may sense a change in thought or sentiment, but not be sure who the specific individuals are who have changed their viewpoint. A general question will bring the appropriate answers.

We must always avoid going round the table in rotation.

The success of a chairman's questioning will determine the success of his meeting, for questions and answers are the basis of reflective thinking. Even when thinking as individuals, and not in a group, we cannot be said to be truly thinking unless we have asked ourselves questions and are trying to answer them.

Evaluating Meetings

Is it possible to judge the effectiveness of our discussion meetings? It is possible to determine whether the meeting is succeeding or not in relation to our purpose. To determine whether the meeting is effective, we can ask ourselves:

"Is the subject reasonably appreciated by the group?"

Reasonable appreciation of the subject implies knowing exactly what the subject is, knowing the situation that gives rise to it, and having sufficient information to start discussing it.

If there is a sense of strangeness, of lack of understanding, or of confusion as the meeting progresses, there is most likely no true appreciation of the subject. Failure to grasp the subject may be because the members attending the meeting are not suitable—do not possess the necessary qualifications to discuss the matter intelligently. Most often appreciation of the subject depends on the leader of the discussion. If the subject is one which is of interest to the group, or in which interest can be developed, there is no reason why it cannot be grasped.

If confusion persists, the leader must ask himself whether he has expressed the subject sufficiently clearly, has given sufficient information, and has asked appropriate questions to stimulate thought about the subject. Obviously if there are acrimonious exchanges, relationships are not satisfactory.

Relationship with Leader

Most important is the relationship between the leader and the members of the group. The group must not lack confidence in the leader. His relationship with members is not satisfactory for purposes of intelligent discussion in the following situations—

1. if he behaves like a teacher with a class;
2. if he asserts his superiority and leans heavily on authority;
3. if he gives too many opinions of his own, stifling the comments of others;
4. if he allows personal exchanges;
5. if he moves too slowly or too quickly.

If there is an unrestrained dominant member, or if there is concentration by the group on one member, then again relationships are not satisfactory.

Checking Summaries

The acceptability of summaries must be examined.

A leader often assumes that his summary is acceptable, without checking to make certain. Remember that any conclusion reached at a discussion meeting must be a co-ordination of the best contributions from each individual's thinking, knowledge and experience. The conclusion is not only acceptable to the meeting, but created by the meeting. Therefore alert members will listen to the summary closely and must be given an opportunity for criticism of it and correction of it. The leader must ask for a check of his summary. He must check by questioning. This check should apply, equally, to the summaries preceding the intermediate conclusions, and to any summarized statements that may be made from time to time by the leader.

Difficult Members and Embarrassing Subjects

We cannot leave our examination of some of the factors that upset a meeting without briefly referring to two other sources of disturbances: difficult members and embarrassing or delicate subjects.

A difficult member is a man who—

1. Talks too much or at length.

2. Constantly talks off the subject, and is generally quite illogical.

3. Is impatient and wants a decision without a thorough investigation.

4. Is unwilling to consider alternatives or compromise; talks only in terms of his own interests versus other people's interests.

5. Makes dogmatic, unsupported statements; gives no reasons; makes points which need clarification or illustration.

6. Engages in personal duels with "opponents"; ignores the group and leader; likes to win an argument rather than solve a problem.

7. Has to "score" against the other members to feel important; does not help create understanding, goodwill and co-operation, but stirs up feelings of antagonism as though in opposition.

8. Does not pay attention; whispers, bothers, interrupts.

By use of questions the leader can go a long way towards disciplining such a member—with committee support. The leader can often restate the main question or topic, and ask the members if discussion isn't becoming irrelevant.

Difficult members often show temperaments and attitudes which delay progress at a meeting, by "colouring" facts and obstructing reasoning. If more than one difficult member is causing this handicap—if the leader finds that emotions are particularly strong—he should change the meeting from one for problem-solving or information-sharing to one for ventilating attitudes and feelings. He might even be advised at times to adjourn the meeting for a "cooling off" period. Often the leader can anticipate the prejudices or vested interests of certain members, and prepare to bring out facts that will challenge any bigoted attitudes.

Embarrassing subjects that cause tension or an unwillingness or fear to talk might be—

1. Matters involving criticism of management or company policies.

2. Comparisons that do not do credit to the company.

3. Revealing situations that reflect badly on a member of the group.

4. A comparison of the value of different individuals (or functions) to the company.

5. Inaugurating new practices which are contrary to someone's "pet" ideas.

A leader can often meet the challenge of "pet" ideas by saying that if these ideas or procedures are good and have stood the test of time, they will stand the test of criticism. A sincere member of a discussion meeting cannot defend pet ideas except on their merits. And these merits must be revealed to the meeting.

A leader must make members feel that they are free to bring their thoughts into the open. Some people are afraid to speak their minds, even though their ideas might help to solve a difficulty and so help the company.

Distribution of Discussion

A leader often takes upon himself the burden of answering all the queries and critical comments submitted by members.

Gradually he finds himself taking up a defensive attitude, or engaging in two-party conversations with individual members. As a result of doing too much of the talking himself, and not always giving good answers to the questions asked, the meeting can tend to become a bored one. The position is worsened when the leader expects acceptance of his statements because he is leader of the discussion.

When a leader does assume this burden of giving most of the answers, and of evaluating most of the contributions, the meeting becomes a full and apathetic one.

This is the pattern—

POOR DISTRIBUTION

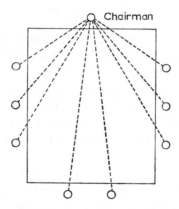

Instead of attempting to give all the answers, the leader should frequently turn a question to a member of the group for an answer—giving the meeting the benefit of that member's knowledge and experience. The leader can then ask some other member to comment on the answer. He can ask for and receive opinions confirming or opposing those expressed.

Participation by all members of a meeting must result in a livelier and more interesting meeting. Very often a pounding of the talk by a leader to "discipline" errant members, or to arouse interest, is tantamount to an admission of dismal failure.

The pattern of discussion is then this—

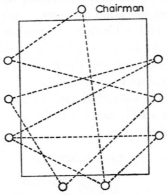

GOOD DISTRIBUTION

Good distribution promotes full participation and keeps the meeting alert and keen. Poor distribution can lead only to tediousness and lack of interest.

As members at a meeting we must always attempt to make the most sincere and effective contributions to the discussion.

Three types of member contributions are—

enquiry; informative (stating facts and reasoned views); persuasive.

The persuasive form of contribution should not be encouraged. It is apt to be too emotional. A leader can often avoid the earnest, persuasive form of talk, by restating it in terms of information.

Participation

A participating member would do well to ask himself the following questions before volunteering statements—

What is the purpose of my comments?
Will they help the meeting to understand the situation being discussed?
Will they help to make a previous comment more complete or more revealing?

Will they help the group to think more critically, more analytically?

Have I information or experience that will help members to clarify their understanding?

These self-seeking questions will keep volunteer contributions relevant, and enable a member to make valuable contributions. A good leader will create confidence in a member, and make him realize that he has information and experience which, if offered, will help members to clarify their understanding.

Formal Chairmanship

Any chairmanship is improved by practice.

PERSONAL REQUIREMENTS OF THE CHAIRMAN

1. Friendliness.
2. Self-control.
3. Efficiency.
4. Clear thought.
5. Knowledge of procedure.
6. Platform-speaking ability.

A chairman must know the business on an agenda, and so be in a position to put different sides of a question to the meeting. He must control the meeting to enable it to arrive at sound decisions without waste of time. He must create and maintain an atmosphere that will influence the meeting to good behaviour.

The manner in which he exercises his function is an example to the meeting. There should be no inconsequence or fussiness. He should always speak up clearly and emphatically.

RIGHTS AND DUTIES OF THE CHAIRMAN

1. Keep order.
2. Make certain that the meeting is properly conducted, and that the sense of the meeting is ascertained. He will

follow the business as set out in the agenda; settle the order of debate and priority of the speakers; rule motions and amendments in or out of order.

3. Determine questions of procedure.

4. Act in the interests of all present at the meeting. The chairman usually derives his authority from the meeting over which he presides.

5. Use his casting vote.

6. Convene a meeting which he considers necessary or urgent.

A FORMAL PUBLIC MEETING

The chairman must—

1. Welcome meeting.
2. Read motion (if any) and arouse interest in the subject.
3. Introduce speaker.
4. Refer to question time.

The chairman must also be prepared to deal with hecklers.

FORMAL COMMITTEES

A chairman here requires *tact, patience*, and *knowledge* of the business to be transacted. He must know the agenda thoroughly and not have to rely on the secretary to get him over difficulties. He should adhere to punctuality and to the order of items on the agenda.

Informality

It is possible at a committee meeting to relax some of the formalities necessary at a general or public meeting. But to relax these formalities is not to abuse them. The chairman must keep control of his committee, checking all irrelevant interruptions. It is wrong to regard formal motions "out of place" at a committee meeting. The *wording* of a motion is of the highest importance. He should crystallize the ideas and opinions of the committee in specific, concrete sentences.

Close

It is sometimes usual for a committee member to bring up an important matter at the end of the meeting, when members are tired or have left, in order to get a motion passed quickly and with little opposition. This is a trick which should be guarded against.

A chairman must close his committee meeting properly so that members will know clearly whether any talk subsequent to the business is "off the record." This may save embarrassment.

A speaker is entitled to speak without interruption, so long as his speech is relevant. If he is not relevant, the chairman must call him to order. In fact, anyone attending the meeting may call attention to a point of order; the chairman then decides the point.

A motion is a proposition upon which people can vote "for" or "against." Hence the importance of clear wording. A motion duly passed at a meeting is considered a resolution of that meeting. Anyone introducing a motion has the right of reply following the debate. The motion must be seconded.

FORMAL RULES

When a motion is before a meeting, a person may move— an amendment; the previous question; the closure; to consider the next business; to adjourn the debate; to adjourn the meeting.

Amendment

1. An amendment must not be in the form of a negative;
2. an amendment is usually seconded. The chairman is mostly unwilling to ask the meeting to consider a proposal supported by only one person;
3. it must be relevant to the motion;
4. it must be moved before the main question is submitted to the vote;
5. it may add certain words to the motion; substitute certain words; omit part of the motion;

6. the proposer of the amendment should, if possible, hand it in written form to the chairman;

7. the proposer of the amendment has no right of reply;

8. once the amendment is formally submitted, the proposer can only withdraw it if the meeting is willing.

An amendment cannot be moved by any person who has proposed the original motion or has spoken on it. But he can, of course, speak when the amendment is before the meeting.

Previous Question

This motion would be, "That the question be not now put." It may be moved by any person who has not spoken on the main question. It must be seconded. It cannot be moved if an amendment is being debated. If this motion is lost, the main question is immediately put to the meeting. If carried, the original question cannot be further discussed at the meeting. Moving the previous question means that the meeting must first (or, in other words "previously") decide whether the main question shall be put at all.

Closure

This motion would be, "That the question be now put" or "That the vote be now taken."

The closure is a motion which need not be seconded. If carried, the main question or the amendment must be immediately submitted. The chairman must be satisfied that there has been free discussion. If lost, the debate proceeds in the ordinary way.

That the Meeting now Considers the Next Business

When an amendment is under discussion, to move the previous question is not allowable; but it will be in order to move "that the meeting proceed to the next business." One effect of the passing of this motion is that the amendment under discussion is dropped, and the original question may continue to be debated.

That the Debate be Adjourned

If this motion is carried the meeting may continue, but the discussion of the particular matter in debate is postponed.

That the Meeting be Adjourned

The effect of this motion will depend on principles governing the meeting. When meetings are called in pursuance of a *legal* duty the chairman cannot adjourn without the permission of the meeting.

This motion must be seconded. It must usually be moved by someone who has not yet spoken.

Voting

Voice	Poll
Show of hands	Division
Ballot	
Proxy	

Annual General Meeting

The Annual General meeting usually follows this form—

1. Apologies for Absence.
2. Minutes.
3. Address by Chairman.
4. Reports.
5. Adoption of Reports.
6. Recommendations suggested or for ratification.
7. Other business.

Conclusion

Let us always recognize that meetings, whatever their nature, are invaluable means for promoting personal understanding and tolerance; understanding of objectives and policies; understanding and tolerance of other people's needs and desires.

Leaders of meetings have a great responsibility; the responsibility to ensure that every meeting realizes its many opportunities of increasing understanding and extending goodwill. This will always call for effort and discipline. Chairmanship or leadership is not a casual function; it involves the obligation to stimulate sound thinking and sound judgements, intelligent discussion and mutual confidence.

To inspire co-operation in thought must be to inspire co-operation in action.

7 Itemizing Talk at and Recording the Resolutions and Recommendations of a Meeting

A Note on Agenda and Minutes

ONE can hardly talk about the nature of a meeting without a note on agenda and minutes. Agenda and minutes are quite normal. They are customarily thought of however, as "items for discussion" and as recording resolutions or the sense of the meeting. The common view of agenda and minutes, and the form in which they are presented, will not be maintained in this general outline of communication. Meetings have already been given a character different from that usually prevailing. In the same way, agenda and minutes will have to be different. The agenda will have to stimulate the type of participation called for at the meetings described, and minutes will have to state conclusions of the meeting's answers to main questions.

But agenda and minutes should be presented in a different guise. When one considers long accepted practices and unquestioned concepts of the average meeting, agenda and minutes are orthodox. Let us examine the agenda first and then refer to the minutes in its light.

Agenda

The agenda should not contain items for "discussion." "Discussion" is limitless. As we have seen, "discussion" must include thinking. It is almost impossible to talk effectively on anything that is not an assertion or an answerable question. It is suggested here that an agenda should contain a list of *questions*, not items for "discussion." When a question is asked, it is almost certain that there will be an attempt to answer it.

Where people are invited to contribute agenda, their possible enthusiasm for doing so will be frustrated if they have to ask a question to which an answer is required, for knowledge of the situation or topic to be examined will be severely tested by the need to formulate a question. The necessity to pose questions can indeed be exacting.

If an agenda contains questions, there will always be a specific main question before the members of the committee. It will then be easier for the chairman to divide the main question into a series of minor questions, and he should insist upon an answer to them. In this way, the chairman is able to exercise discipline, and summaries of contributions will be easier to read and more intelligible. The agenda will also be more informative to those who do not or cannot attend the meeting.

Minutes

Similarly, minutes should depart from the orthodox conception of them. Normally, minutes are left to the secretary of the meeting, who draws up what often prove to be "bastard" minutes: they are in effect neither minutes of resolution nor minutes of narration. A secretary of a board committee used to tape-record each meeting. He would then carry the recorder away in order to play back the meeting, and so prepare the minutes! It is difficult to think of a greater waste of time or of energy. If minutes are to have a precise sense, and not merely depend upon the whims and fancies of a particular individual, then they should in effect, be, uttered by the chairman and accepted by the meeting and not merely written by the secretary. A chairman or leader in the process of his intermediate summaries in fact dictates the minutes when he checks acceptance of the summaries. If the meeting assents to the minutes, it has for practical purposes created them. It is then scarcely likely that a meeting will dissipate time at a subsequent session by contesting the minutes of the previous meeting. People do not contest what they have created. Although it is true that a good secretary will frequently compensate for a bad chairman, this is an exceptional circumstance which we shall not deal with now. When a chairman in effect dictates the minutes, the secretary has simply to note the summaries accepted by the meeting and, if he follows the right practice, re-write them in the minutes.

Agenda and minutes may have to carry a procedural form when meetings are shaped by company law requirements. With the average meeting held within industry, or in one of its departments, there will be some departure from orthodoxy. Company law was never intended to apply to the average meeting. It may of course be necessary to apply procedural rules at formal meetings; the law may insist on formality and even speak of its methods of operation.

If the character of a meeting is to be changed, then agenda and minutes must likewise undergo an alteration from their familiar form. Precedent has a value if it achieves a particular purpose, but the average agenda and minutes achieve little purpose and take up a great deal of otherwise useful time.

8 People Meeting to Solve a Personal Problem

A Chapter on Making Joint Consultation Really Effective

IT has often been said that if joint consultation is to work well in industry, it is necessary that workers' representatives should know how to make it effective. While this is obviously true, we cannot assume that all management representatives know how to maintain a high and efficient standard of discussion.

Representation means talking and thinking. These jobs, in common with all jobs, should be done well. Unfortunately, thinking and talking (arranging and presenting facts and ideas clearly, interestingly and acceptably) are for the most part done badly.

A representative has to impart not only facts and ideas, but attitudes and feelings; he has to gather these from his constituents—often when the latter may even resent having to express them. Having established a commonly agreed point of view, he has to attend the consultative meeting and give a clear picture of his case. He finally reports back to his constituents, enabling them to share in any understanding reached at the meeting. The task, if taken seriously, is not an easy one and calls for careful thought and practice.

When one talks of discussion, one means good discussion. Good discussion is more than conversation round a table. General conversation may promote good fellowship and yet not solve problems. As one workers' representative put it:

"There is no point in creating friendly relations for the sake of doing so. Workers are hard-headed enough to know that everything should have a purpose. We have little time for joint consultation which does not lead to increased efficiency."

If discussion is to lead to increased efficiency, it has itself to be efficient—which means that it has to become a disciplined, *technically* thorough and able job, and not merely the chit-chat of spinster aunts round a tea-kettle. If we are to improve our techniques, we must regard discussion speaking as a scientific means of exchanging ideas and weighing and settling problems.

Thinking

Discussion suggests, too, collective *thinking*. And "thinking" must be distinguished from reverie or day-dreaming and idle contemplation. We think about a thing when we have a special purpose for doing so, when we want to arrive at decisions or solve problems. It calls among other disciplines for the collection of facts, the ability to examine them as evidence of something other than themselves, and the ability, without the interference of our emotions or prejudices, to draw conclusions from them.

In *individual* thinking we "think out" matters alone. In *collective* thinking we pool facts and ideas: and so we get facts which we did not know about; we get ideas which begin to affect our own, and yet further ideas are suggested to us by the remarks of others. And so in joint consultation we should arrive nearer to good solutions for the better and happier performance of our jobs.

Logic

But these good solutions are possible only if we realize that joint consultative discussion is allied with logic, with reflective thinking, rather than with emotional or persuasive activity. That means relying on our intelligence rather than on our feelings, being able to distinguish what a person *thinks* from what he *feels*.

A representative's job may be divided into three stages—

1. talking (where possible) to his constituents; getting the facts; discovering thoughts, feelings and attitudes; reaching agreement on an overall picture of the situation or problem;

2. participation at the meeting;

3. reporting back: telling constituents of the conditions reached, and why they were reached. The success of reporting back depends on the success with which the representative entered into the problem with his constituents at the first stage.

Let us try to analyse the representative's work at each stage, remembering, of course, that his activity is qualified by the size of his organization and of his constituency.

FIRST STAGE: *discussing the problem or situation with his constituents*
The work here involves—

1. getting the facts;
2. fitting the facts together and clarifying the issues;
3. getting opinions and feelings;
4. noting what actions are recommended;
5. encouraging discussion on the advantages and disadvantages of each suggestion;
6. getting decisions on how the actions suggested will affect individuals, the group, production;
7. summing up the general view, and making certain that the group agrees with the summary.

Getting views is not merely a matter of asking for them. Men are of many kinds: easy-going, unfriendly, efficient, lazy, ambitious; and man is not primarily a reasoning but an emotional being. His first question on any occasion is usually: "What is there in this for me"? A representative should know the thoughts and feelings of his fellows, and their relation to one another and to their superiors. It is always important to recognize how far opinion is based on prejudice or resentment and how far on reason.

Discussion with one's constituents before a meeting is in itself a form of joint consultation, with the representative in the position of a chairman. He should make people "stick" to facts and principles and keep personalities out of the discussion.

SECOND STAGE: *participation at the meeting*

If his function at the first stage is properly carried out, the representative comes to the meeting with a full picture of the agreed view of his constituents.

The meeting is not merely a matter of arguing or debating. A debater is a person who has already made up his mind and tries to convince or persuade others to accept his point of view. A discussion aims to analyse a problem and then to solve it, dealing with questions about which people have not conclusively made up their minds.

As the aim of consultation is a practical one—action—the investigation of a problem must be carried out in a proper spirit of research.

1. The problem or "felt" difficulty is clearly stated;

2. the various issues are clarified (one of the main causes of futile discussion is a broad or vague statement of issues; and there must be no uncertain or confusing words);

3. the issues being stated, the causes and results of them are examined;

4. possible solutions are proposed, and the practical advantages and disadvantages of each are considered;

5. the solution that appears to be the best is selected, and so reaches the status of a conclusion;

6. action is formulated to complete the process of policy.

The Chairman

Of course no disciplined activity at a meeting is possible without a knowledgeable and efficient chairman. He must—

1. get to know the individuals in his consultative group as well as possible;

2. maintain a friendly atmosphere;

3. protect people from personal criticism and hurt feelings;

4. not give the impression that he is allowing preference or prejudice to override sound decision;

5. fully know the subject to be discussed, and be able to isolate and analyse a problem;

6. assemble the facts and evaluate them;

7. give useful information which the group may need;

8. encourage interesting and informative questions and replies;

9. accurately repeat queries addressed;

10. interpret what is not clearly understood;

11. guarantee genuine discussion and freedom from disputation or wrangling;

12. not capitalize on the first good lead;

13. generally invite and encourage talk, but "keep it on the beam": there must be no irrelevances;

14. summarize points and conclusions with completeness and accuracy; and before the meeting breaks up, make sure that there is general acceptance and understanding.

THIRD STAGE: *Reporting back*

Reporting back, if properly done, serves a dual purpose: it not only communicates the conclusions of a meeting, but conveys the true value of consultation as a medium for solving common problems. Much of a worker's apathy towards joint consultation rises from a doubt about its efficiency and a suspicion of its motives. If he is brought fully into the picture by his representative before and after a meeting, he will at least feel that he has every opportunity to share in the procedure.

Assuming that the representative has properly consulted with his constituents in the first stage, his function when reporting back is to show—

1. how their view differed from the general view;
2. what the added facts were;
3. what the differing views and ideas were;
4. what several solutions were suggested, and what were the advantages and disadvantages of each;
5. what the final solution is and the reasons for it. He should invite comment from his fellows to clear up any misunderstanding.

Some of the duties of a representative here suggested are not always possible. This is clearly realized. Face-to-face contact with all constituents in large organizations is not often practicable. Where minutes are substantially relied upon, they should always be attractively set out, and written in simple, intelligible language. The spoken word is, of course, preferable to the written word, and certainly more impressive.

But whatever the degree to which full consultation with constituents is possible, a representative—whether on an advisory committee or on a committee empowered to make decisions—should realize that his job calls for a disciplined and systematic approach to the problem of effective joint consultation.

9 Talking to People

A Chapter on the Efficacy of all Speaking

Platform Speaking

The term "public" speaking is not a favourite of the author of this book. All speaking is in a sense "public" speaking, because there is always somebody present when we talk. "Private" speaking is, in the last resort, speaking to oneself. Such a person requires our sympathy, or one might even be alarmed by him.

The subject of speaking is so important, however, and its significance so great, that it is difficult to do proper justice to it.

Having stated that "public" speaking is probably a misnomer, which can lead many otherwise able and experienced people to the purchase of a number of frightening books on "public" speaking, one should now say what are not the implications of the term. It does not imply merely an ability to speak with confidence, it does not merely imply an unselfconscious ease of manner on a platform or a willingness to speak without fear on any occasion. In short, speech education does not consist in platform exhibitionism.

We may note that the advantages to be gained from consideration of speech education are not only educational but personal. The personal advantages, especially with constant practice, are that—

1. a person will think more clearly;
2. he will improve his appearance;
3. he will improve his voice;

4. he will improve his powers of concentration;

5. he will widen his interests.

By examining speech education a man or woman will be helped—

1 *In Industry or Commerce*

(*a*) in meetings;

(*b*) in talks to small or large audiences;

(*c*) in giving instructions;

(*d*) in writing letters and reports;

(*e*) in giving expression to special knowledge and experience.

2 *In Community Life*

(*a*) in talking about general and social problems;

(*b*) in politics;

(*c*) in conversation and social relationships.

There is no mystery about effective speaking and getting one's ideas across to one's fellows. To speak clearly and concisely is at the same time an art and a craft. It is not an art inborn, or an attribute of only a few; practically anyone, with intelligent application, can determine to express himself forcefully and convincingly. "Public" speaking is not a matter of studied gestures and "elocution" voice; it requires a direct, simple, straightforward manner without tricks of oratory or declamation.

SPEAKER AND AUDIENCE

Let us consider the two components of *speaker* and *audience*. A speaker's problems are different from a writer's, although both use verbal symbols. A writer depends on syntax. The order with which his words are put down suggest intonation, pause and emphasis. A speaker brings his whole personality and possible behaviour with him on to the platform to reinforce the words and ideas expressed by him. His behaviour on the platform, or for that matter in the arm-chair, will add to or detract from the value of his utterance.

In general, his effectiveness results from a combination of separate skills: word selection, personality, behaviour, adaptation to audience, and so on. The speaker has first to form desirable attitudes towards language, towards his organization for accurate or persuasive utterance of ideas. Adaptation to an audience demands, of course, appropriate selection of language.

A speaker should know something, obviously, of the psychological value of words, be able to invoke the accep-tance of persuasion and/or arouse any particular emotional attitude that he may require.

There are four main methods of delivering a speech—

1. writing out a speech and reading it;
2. writing out a speech and committing it to memory;
3. extempore method;
4. a combination of the above.

WRITING OUT THE SPEECH AND READING IT

It would be incorrect to say that writing out the speech and reading it has no benefits. It has obvious initial benefits as disciplinary *practice* in coherence and clear utterance. Apart from this value, however, this method of preparing and delivering a speech is probably the worst method possible. It is bad in the first place because we do not speak as we write. Writing, which gives more time for careful selection of words, may lead to developing sentences that are involved, and sound stilted. In any event, it is very difficult to listen to a person who reads; often his sentences are too long. The audience may be trying to determine the sense of his last sentence when he is already well on the way to completing the next sentence.

In most instances, writing out the speech and reading it deprives the speech of directness and vitality. The imagery is apt to be worked out with intricate contrast, while climax is artificial. Any departure from the direct, conversational fluency which should mark a good speech will always tire an audience and render it inattentive and restless. If one may use a popular expression: "the speech smells of the lamp" and it loses most of its power.

Loss of the Power of the Eye

A speaker who reads his speech from a manuscript must sacrifice "the power of the eye." Eyes are the most important of the *means* of expression, and may often produce subtle effects. All changes in this expression are lost to the audience when a speaker has to confine his eyes to a manuscript.

Further, such a speaker cannot possibly control his audience when reading. He is unaware of their non-verbal reactions to what he is saying. Every audience has restless or inattentive members. Often a glance might bring them back to attention, before the restlessness infectiously spreads to other parts of the audience.

Vocal Flexibility Lost

The greatest disadvantage of reading, perhaps, is that the voice in reading is entirely different from its manner in conversation or direct speaking. In conversation the voice is characterized by variety. In reading the voice is rather level toned, without many marked changes. Even the best of readers find it difficult to avoid a monotonous pitch or timing which may control the voice when conveying thought from the printed page.

Apart from this, the voice is generally cramped and misdirected when reading. The voice is aimed at the manuscript or the floor, rather than out towards the audience. Because of the position of the head, the muscles of the throat and upper chest are constricted. In this way resonance and carrying power are lessened.

In learned societies and conferences a "paper" is often read. Despite what has been said about the need at times to read technical information, it is always a pity when reading actually takes place. As the talk is circulated as a rule anyway, the point of reading it becomes less important. It would be much better if, having circulated the talk, a speaker had merely to talk *on* his paper, and if possible talk extempore. He will, in this way, limit himself to a few explanatory assertions. The audience would be much more provoked, and as a consequence probably ask him more enlightened questions.

A certain industrialist, no doubt well known to some readers, wanted to get support for a management project in Britain. He wrote out a speech in the privacy of his Thames valley home and hawked it around. England, Scotland, Wales and Ireland were all the recipients of the one paper. Apart from England, all the countries were most annoyed— they felt that the "speech" had very little application to them; the idea of adaptation had simply not, for some reason, occurred to the industrialist concerned.

Reading is often the Best Method

Apart from these disadvantages there must be times when the reading of a carefully prepared address is probably the best. For example, eminent political leaders often write out and read their speeches to avoid being misquoted. Technical addresses, involving figures and statistics, have at times regretfully to be written out.

WRITING OUT THE SPEECH AND COMMITTING IT TO MEMORY

This method has many of the faults found in the method of writing and reading. The language used is probably artificial; the sentence structure is involved; and the speaker's voice is likely to lack variety. Actually, the result is simply that a mental page is substituted for a real page. The staring eyes of many speakers will testify to this.

Writing out a speech and memorizing it only leads to an emphasis on "nerves." Everybody is nervous, and it is quite stupid to believe that one can be cured of nerves. Even a tooth has to be injected before the nerve in it is dead. Nerves should be conceived as part of one's environment to be overcome with practice. In fact, not to feel nervous might mean, as every actor knows, a dismal performance. However, speaking from memory is apt to exaggerate "nerves," and one need not be reminded of the churning stomach, the stiff knees, the dry mouth. The likelihood of an attack of "nervousness" is greater when the speech has been memorized.

No Chance for Adaptation to Audience

Again, no chance is given in a speech written out and committed to memory to consider unexpected circumstances in the audience. The speech is delivered hastily, as it was committed to memory. If any changes are necessary, or heckling takes place, the association of ideas, by which the sentences may be remembered, is destroyed. After any kind of interruption, it is often impossible to pick up the right thread of the discourse again.

Little Reformulation of Thought

Naturally the audience does not react as a whole when a speaker holds forth. The mind is occupied in remembering words and sentences, and the speaker cannot give sufficient attention, perhaps, when the need arises, to reformulating the thought at the time it is uttered.

A Speech may be Forgotten

The memory is not always reliable, and there is hardly a speaker who uses the "memory" style who has not gone through the unnerving experience of forgetting. If a single word in a sentence chances to be changed, the verbal associations are broken up and it is often impossible for the speaker to go on. Once a speaker has forgotten a speech, he will always have the fear that a similar experience will be his in the future. As a result he cannot do his best work, for part of his attention is on his speech and part of it on the fear of forgetting.

THE EXTEMPORE METHOD

This is the best method. It involves a carefully-prepared outline, the nature of which we shall examine in a moment, so that the speaker knows beforehand just what ideas he will express; but he leaves the exact language in which these ideas will be uttered until he delivers his speech.

Impromptu speaking should be distinguished. By this is meant that the speaker prepares neither ideas nor words before he actually speaks. In the extempore method the ideas are never left to the moment; the speaker knows his goal, and the means he will use to reach it.

Nevertheless, we often speak *impromptu* in the course of business. For example, when one speaks on a telephone, or is asked a question, one can be said to be speaking impromptu when one gives the answer.

Notes

Whether or not notes should be revealed to an audience depends, of course, upon the individual, and the possible complexity of his outline. If the speaker finds it easy to carry an outline in his mind, so much the better for him. On the other hand, if a speaker finds difficulty in remembering an outline, there can be no harm in having notes on the platform.

Notes should be Properly Prepared and Properly Used

No attempt should be made to conceal one's notes. They need not be "hidden," particularly behind the speaker. His contortions are apt to be somewhat upsetting.

The notes should preferably be written on one side of a postcard. The writing should be large enough to allow the speaker to read the sentences clearly. Nothing is more upsetting to both speaker and audience than a need to lift cards closely before the eyes in order to examine the language and meaning.

The speaker should not put down words to remind him of what he wants to say, but actual assertions that he intends to make. Once an assertion is clear to the speaker he will soon find words with which to express it. Besides, once a list of assertions is written down it is almost impossible for a speaker, who merely has to glance at his cards, to forget what he wants to say.

Ink should be used in preference to pencil. Writing in pencil, apart from being less incisive, may easily be obliterated.

The main assertions should be underlined, so that they stand out more plainly on the card, thus enabling the speaker to find his points more efficiently. Different coloured inks may be used with advantage.

The assertion should be of some idea. It must be emphasized that words used to remind a speaker of what he wishes to say should be avoided, because they may fail to trigger off his memory.

It is often said that slang and colloquial expressions abound in an extempore speech; that there is repetition and diffuseness in it; that the sentence structure is often primitive; that the grammar is at fault; that the speaker often makes ill-considered statements. All these charges are frequently justified, but the fault lies rather in the practice of the method and not in the method itself. With the right kind of practice these faults will soon be overcome. It may take longer to develop the extempore type of speech, but the freedom which it finally gives to the speaker would alone justify its title to the best of the four methods.

THE COMBINED STYLE

A speaker may write and read in part and speak from memory in part; he may deliver an extempore speech on the whole, but introduce a part in which he relies on memory. The use of the combined style will depend entirely upon persons speaking and the purpose for which they speak.

THE MAIN THOUGHT

When a speaker has determined his purpose, he should write it down. He is then able to decide upon his main thought, which will be found in answering the question: "What thought, placed in the minds of the audience, will most likely accomplish the desired result?" The determination of the main thought of a speech requires a knowledge of the subject in hand, a knowledge, if possible, of the audience, and sufficient knowledge of the method of producing required effects upon people. The conscious production of these effects depends on practice.

The Ancient Greeks regarded rhetoric as being concerned with plausibility and not truth. Clarity of diction was highlighted and not soundness of judgement. Socrates, however, said that the real aim was truth and Aristotle spoke of rhetoric as the art of persuading an audience who cannot grasp a number of arguments in a single view. It is probably best to say that rhetoric, aiming at persuasion, uses both scientific truth and genuine emotion for a practical purpose so it makes a combination of both persuasion and truth.

Main Thought when the Purpose is Action

It is comparatively easy to find a main thought when the purpose is action. The request resolves itself into establishing the one great reason why the audience should act as it is asked to do. Generally, the reason is that the particular course of action will bring some benefit to the audience. If the speaker then establishes the main reason why the course of action will be beneficial, he is more likely to be convincing.

Main Thought when the End is Belief

What has been said when the end is action is equally true when the end is belief. The difference between action and belief is not a great one, or should not be. If a speaker is appealing for belief, he must set down as his main purpose his main thought.

Main Thought when the End is Exposition

In unbiased exposition, it is not easy to speak of the main thought; the only object is to explain something, and do so clearly; but even in explanation there may be a tendency for the ideas to group themselves about a dominant idea. There is usually some purpose behind any exposition. Often the purpose of an exposition may be belief.

If a person is going to make a short speech, he must make his mind up what he is going to say. If he cannot answer the question easily it is because he does not know his purpose.

DELIVERY

Quintilian, who was an ancient Roman and who, apart from his theoretical interest was, no doubt, "tops" as a speechmaker, had this to say: "Delivery is by most authorities true action; but it appears to derive the one name from the voice and the other from gesture. As to the thing itself, it possesses a marvellous power and efficacy in speeches, for it does not so much matter what kind of thoughts we have composed inwardly as it does in what manner they are expressed, since each individual in our audience is moved just as he hears. Much of but moderate quality, if recommended by forceful delivery, will produce a more powerful effect than the most excellent language, if deprived of that advantage.

"Delivery in general depends on two factors, voice and gesture, of which the one appeals to the eyes and the other to the ears. Now, good qualities of voice, like those of all other faculties, are heightened by ability and diminished by carelessness. Therefore let the voice not be relaxed by lack of practice, but let it be braced by use. . . . How much importance gesture has is manifest enough from the simple reflection that it can signify most things even without words."

SUMMARY

1. Everything said must contribute to the purpose. Some speakers seem to think that speaking means uttering all the

thoughts they have on their chosen subject. As has been said: "Such a speaker can be likened to a man who leaves home for an hour's recreation with no idea of where he is going or what sport he will engage in. Consequently he takes with him all of his recreational equipment—golf equipment, tennis equipment, fishing equipment."

2. Every speech should have a clear purpose, and everything in it should contribute to that purpose.

(*a*) The speaker must ask himself, "What is the object of my speech. What result is it to achieve?"

(*b*) He must ask himself what his main thought is, what thought will most likely enable the audience to achieve the desired result.

(*c*) He should convey the main thought, divided into three or four propositions, to the audience, and so make known the desired result.

(*d*) The speaker should give illustrations of each one of these separate propositions. "He who aims at nothing will be almost sure to hit it." More speeches fail from a lack of aim than from any other cause.

Having considered platform speaking, let us now look at conversation.

Speaking to One or More Persons

Conversation is the best preparation we can make for more challenging speech. The freedom and ease of our daily lives creates habits that may well go with us into more formal occasions.

It is quite wrong to think of delivering an effective public speech, and yet talk to people with perhaps bad behaviour and even sloppily. If a person talks one way in public and another in private, he is simply two-faced. When speaking to one or more persons we should, as we know, become aware of our own and other people's language habits. Normally, when words are used in utterance or in writing, the speaker or reader, we have noted, gives a meaning to them common to him, not to the user. We must therefore make our own language habits flexible and adaptable, and know something of the unconscious attitudes towards language and their effects on response and sympathy.

Again, a distinction between informative and evaluative words is particularly important, and the reference of either must be perfectly clear to the listener if we expect competent service.

If anyone develops and elaborates his attitudes towards language this will stand him in immense stead in delivery of a "public" speech. In both instances the speaker should assure himself of the good and sufficient conditions in the use of verbal language and its equivalent that may make our messages acceptable, reaching not only understanding but human sympathy as well.

A speaker, whether in "public" or in "private," should understand what sound thinking means, the meaning of clear statement, value of evidence, and how to conduct a good argument or to present specialized knowledge to people less informed. Many executives seek to improve their abilities, not only as public speakers but as conversationalists. The emphasis on improvement of abilities is wrong, the emphasis should be on practice. Talking is a natural activity if one has common sense. Talking is obviously quite familiar; it only appears strange and difficult when we think about it. When people cannot say clearly what they mean and their thoughts become confused, they are most likely uninterested.

CONCLUSION

To learn to talk better, and so to get better reaction to things we say, we do not require a long treatise or course of instruction; what we want are some elementary principles followed by frequent practice and criticism if it can comfortably be obtained. If we know something of what a listener thinks when he tries to listen, the principles of effective speaking will readily occur—

1. A person wishes to be attracted to what we are saying, and to find that listening is interesting and pleasant. We must recover the good voices we were born with, and develop the habit of articulating words clearly, varying tone and pace for emphasis and expressiveness. A speaker to one or many people should not murmur or mumble or speak in monotonous tones.

2. A listener tries to interpret the meaning of our words and our statements. He wants to find the process of interpretation easy. If it becomes difficult he will cease to listen. We simply have, therefore, to take the trouble to think well and clearly before we speak. If thoughts are vague or uninteresting we are unable to give utterance to them properly.

3. A listener tries to associate what we are saying with his own knowledge and experience. If he cannot do that easily he is not likely to understand us and he will give up trying to do so. It is therefore necessary for a speaker to broaden and deepen his own interests and his appreciation of the interests of other people. In the light of what we know about the next man's interests we can give familiar examples of unfamiliar ideas.

4. A listener is trying to remember what we say. That is why the reader has been urged, when writing a letter or speaking on a platform, to use simple words. The importance of speaking well is a part of the art of living well.

10 Giving Instructions

A Chapter on the Nature of Instructions and Orders

INSTRUCTION is so much part of management practice that any re-examination or reconsideration of it appears to be unnecessary.

But instructions, which are often looked upon as equivalent to a command or order, nevertheless reflect the frequently missed opportunities for expanding morale. Instructions as such should, when given, be a form of training and education.

They are a means of inculcating *habits* of action which will enable an employee to act more often at his own discretion; the Duke of Wellington is said to have exclaimed: "Habit a second nature! Habit is ten times nature."

We must understand the influence instruction as a form of training and education may have. We might emphasize that the improvement of one mental function increases the efficiency of other functions; a mental function improves others because the functions may be, at least in part, identical. As Thorndike and Gates put it in their *Elementary Principles of Education*. "Addition improves multiplication because multiplication is largely addition; knowledge of Latin gives increased ability to learn French because many of the facts learned in the one case are needed in the other; the study of geometry may lead a pupil to be more logical in all respects, for one element of being logical in all respects is to realize that facts can be absolutely proven and to admire and desire the certain and unquestionable source of demonstration."

Instruction and Insight

Where instructions are treated in effect as a form of training and education, the need for orders may well diminish. Instructions must be viewed in the total frame of relationships affecting people's attitudes for better or worse.

If there is to be any insight into a situation calling for the operations ordered, instructions must then be more than simply orders. They must be so written or spoken that an employee can use his or her initiative, observing the demands of a situation before the operation is required.

Sir Stafford Cripps, in an article in *The Times* in 1946, said: "We are entering on a new era of industrial development in which we must concentrate more and more on that delicate instrument, the human machine."

It is, of course, with the human machine that instructions are concerned. Although the trouble in industry may be that it does have human beings, and management may pray for complete automation to arrive, we have at present to deal with people, co-ordinate their activity and inspire co-operation and initiative. If we must do this then the trouble taken over instructions is well worth while. But, "What matters is not what is said," wrote Guy Hunter in *Studies in Management*, "or how it is said, but how it is heard." To be truly effective, instructions have to be adapted to the interests and attitudes of the person to whom they are addressed.

Workers are most loyal when they have pride in their work and in their supervisor. Management often increases this pride by developing the attractiveness of the employee's environment. It must also concern itself at least with the nature of instructions. An attractive impression of the company may develop a sense of identification with it. Management must be more than sensitive to welfare, however, and must use the instruction as a means of instilling the right kind of motivation.

OPERATIONAL DEFINITION

If ever operational definition—definition in terms of operations and actions—was necessary, instruction points to its suitable and profitable use. This is where the relation between words and the reality or events referred to, or to which they are intended to refer, does matter. An instruction is meant to get a person or persons to perform a required act, perhaps to apply to it a special skill, and to do so competently.

It becomes a matter, therefore, of the utmost importance that direction is immediately indicated, and the essentials of the job are known; it would be even better if the special knowledge of the employee were motivated to dictate suitable action to him. It is best that any order should *occur* to a responsible employee and not have to be uttered in a ringing tone.

It seems puzzling that something so vital as an instruction should be left to the traditional practice of a supervisor or manager without training; or possibly without a safe knowledge of the relationship between words and the action they intend.

Qualification in semantics, or the science of language, is naturally not being advocated. An appreciation of the human load already upon a manager would preclude yet a further qualification, and in this instance a fairly remote one, being required of him. Operational definition, in the sense given, is a purely practical process calling for little skill other than constant performance.

The duty to know is less on the person receiving the instruction than on the person who gives it. This is not to say that there is no burden of intelligent listening on the receiver. There is, and most people do not listen well. But the major onus lies on the person giving the instruction; and he has to make it so clear that misunderstanding is impossible.

Don Quixote said to Sancho in Cervantes' book: "Liberty, Sancho, is one of the most valuable gifts Heaven has

9—(B.648)

bestowed upon men; the treasures which the earth encloses, or the sea covers, are not to be compared with it. Life may, and ought to be, risked for liberty, as well as for honour; and, on the contrary, slavery is the greatest evil that can befall us." An employee *must* have insight into the circumstances creating the demand. He must enjoy that freedom of mind which will allow alternatives in the performance of a job.

A Foreman and Instruction

The improper use of instruction will affect a foreman as surely as will failure to operate within a budget. It is, of course, of importance to the foreman to know when to use suggestion, or directions and commands. To offer suggestions implies that the foreman has confidence in the employee's judgement; that the latter and the foreman are pooling their experiences in order to work out the best possible method of doing the job. Similarly, instructions must be so improved that insight into the total situation is possible; this will do more even than suggestions to develop ideas and knowledge in the performance of a job.

One would hope that the foreman would, at least sometimes, use the suggestion method of getting jobs done; but the most effective device for the building of morale is to look upon *instruction as a form of dissemination of knowledge*. The foreman who makes full use of this device does recognize the talent in his individual subordinates, and thus develop them to become still more effective on the job. "A willing bird flies farther than a thrown stone."

It is true that the utterance of positive statements, indicating exactly what has to be done, may yet leave the impression that the employee is again without the opportunity to express his own ideas or to pool his experience. Where this happens the fault lies in the *practice* of giving instructions, not in the *principle* of making them more informative.

The foreman who has the respect of his workers will have no difficulty in the use of instructions as they have been described. In Robert Louis Stevenson's *Treasure Island:* " 'Wot's wot?' repeated one of the buccaneers in a deep growl. 'Ah, he'd be a lucky one as knowed that'." This comment of the buccaneer has a direct application to the average instruction given, certainly by middle management.

One might even apply Dante's opening phrase of the *Commedia:*

> "Midway upon the journey of our life
> I found myself within a forest dark,
> For the straightforward pathway had been lost."

Although Dante obviously wrote in quite a different context, his comment still has relevance to our use of the word "instruction."

Professional Employees

The problem of suitable instructions becomes particularly acute when we consider the specialist, the technologist and the scientist in industry. The fact remains that the technologist and scientist simply cannot be treated like any other employee.

Whereas the traditional industrial organization must establish a direct relationship between rank and power, large numbers of highly qualified technologists and scientists might well interfere with this relationship. The majority of scientists and technologists in any particular organization do not necessarily have rank conferred upon them.

Normally, of course, an organization sees that ability is awarded with appropriate promotion. The implication is that individuals of lower rank have lesser abilities.

In the development of research, industry has increasingly brought scientific and technological manpower into its organizations. This has been done, however, with the usual relationship of rank and power still existing. In other words, the technologists and scientists were brought into the labour force as if they were yet another group of employees; they experience low prestige in the industrial organization. This condition is at the moment undergoing, as it should do, reasonable change.

The kinds of authority encountered by the scientist and technologist in industry are different from the kinds of authority met in a university. The usual industrial organization has a system of authority based on occupation of an office; and the industrial laboratory may reflect this kind of practice.

Generally the authority of an executive is mainly the result of his occupying a particular position, and this authority is only slightly based, if at all, on his knowledge and experience. To organize well the new intake entering industry at the present time, there must be a change from our usual conception of managerial responsibility in order to understand and express the meaning of professional authority.

If an instruction given to these specialists is to be permissive rather than authoritative, then management must be detailed and precise in its instruction-giving; it must outline the situation creating the need for the operation concerned.

Conclusion

Instructions must stimulate appropriate attitudes at the same time as they inform, motivating operatives to willing and co-ordinated effort. The problem of instruction-giving, which is at the heart of technical communication in industry, will then prove helpful in the superior-subordinate relationship at every level in an organization.

Even if one looks upon an instruction as a command, one should remember that a command should really be a piece of information. A command, however, may be said normally to produce a reflex action or an immediate submission of the will, without any thought attending it. It may still encounter the resistance of wills, and get, as a consequence, an aggressive reaction not originally intended.

There are many ways in which men can communicate with one another. They can engage in gestures, cries, words, pictures or write letters. When for any reason, as with foreign workers, people cannot talk together by word of mouth, they take to conversing in gestures—in what is called "dumb show" or pantomime. It is really astonishing that this gestural conversation is effective, and can be said to be cleverly accomplished.

11 Communication by the Written Word

A Chapter on the Writing of Letters

THIS chapter will be short, as it is not worth while engaging in repetitions and so proving tiresome to readers. Enough has been said about letters, to make it unnecessary to repeat counsels which may have now become truisms. Many books or chapters have been devoted to the art of letter-writing, and there is no intention here of stressing the obvious. It does seem, on the other hand, that one has to be obvious in the whole field of communication, if only to *systematize* obviousness. It is important at all events to consider this topic against the general background of communication.

All letters must be written, as indeed all communication must occur, spontaneously. The secretary taking down the shorthand notes should be an intermediary for *spontaneous* address by the writer to his reader. The writer of a letter should write simply. Simplicity, however, is more than a matter of simple words; simple language is *the* language of information, and may thus well reflect the kind of spontaneity demanded. This means, among other things, that to avoid being stilted one should avoid all business jargon, and what the Americans call "gobbledy-gook."

It is important besides to be careful about the beginning of a letter and the end of it. Nothing is a greater waste of time than to say that the writer "assures the reader of his best attention at all times." The assumption here is that the reader will then say to himself "awfully decent fellow, what!" He probably does not even read this kind of meaningless phraseology.

Very often at the beginning of a letter the writer "adverts to." Why he cannot simply say, "I have read your letter of so-and-so date" is beyond understanding. Having "adverted to," the writer then *repeats* the query or information in the letter he has received, as though the memory of the sender were quite hopelessly impaired. It is sufficient, assuming there is an appropriate heading, for the writer to reply to the letter received by saying, for example: "Certainly I can do what you ask me; I hope to let you have the finished product within a couple of weeks."

The important thing is to avoid a repetitive beginning and a meaningless ending to a letter. The end of a letter leaves the final impression. Avoid weak and insincere pleasantries such as "Thanking you in anticipation," "awaiting your reply," "assuring you of our best attention at all times," "trusting this matter will have the attention of your good selves," "awaiting the favour of your esteemed command," "we beg to remain." Such phrases are not courteous. Courtesy is something that arises from the whole *tone* of a letter.

The Heading

The title or heading of a letter is of great importance, for a name probably indicates the contents. Therefore one might put:

Dear Sir,
                    Your contract 25th June, 1967

The reader of the letter will immediately know what the letter is about. He does not need to be told this in an opening paragraph, which usually exhausts and confuses him before he gets to the main point. Very often, indeed, the main point of a letter is lost because the reader is simply not sure what the main point is. It may be noted that one can come to the point in question and be direct and brief without being brusque. "Terse" does not mean "discourteous." There is always a tendency to confuse verbosity with courtesy.

As letter-writers our first duty, then, is to avoid hackneyed, meaningless expressions and commercial jargon; these waste time and dissipate thought. As J. B. Opdyke expresses it in *Take a Letter, Please:* "When letters were written with a goose quill it was perhaps in keeping to begin them with 'I-now-take-my-pen-in-hand,' and it was expected that there should be such lineal descendants as *'replying-to-your-enquiry-of'*; *'in-reply-I-would-say'*; *'enclosed-herewith'*; *'attached-hereto'*; *'hoping-to-receive'*; *'as-per.'* These and their brother bromides are proved to be worthless, wasteful, business-destroying debris. It is an impertinence to blur and bungle so precious a thing as human thought with this sort of thing: 'In reply to your communication of the 26th inst. regarding so-and-so . . . I beg to be permitted to say that. . . .' Here are some twenty useless words which must be read before the meat of the matter (if any) is digested. They disgust the alert business man who must read them." Letters are increasing in importance, and cannot be squandered in the use of absurd phrases.

Reason for a Letter

Primarily a letter is written, apart from possibly forming part of a contract, for the receiver to carry out instructions and/or to record significant facts. This may involve giving information or asking for it. A letter must be precisely written in order to inform clearly. A letter may be a reply to a letter received or it may be a letter that calls for a reply. Ask yourself—

1. Is my letter a specific reply to the *questions* asked? and
2. Will my reader know from my letter precisely *what he must reply to?*

Qualities of a Letter

1. Simplicity.
2. Clarity and precision.
3. Courtesy (that is, being agreeable, creating the impression of service, friendliness and co-operation).
4. Terseness (excluding everything that is not relevant).
5. Force (the emphasis is on freshness and sincerity).

Examples of the Clumsy Use of English

Do not say	*Say instead*
"We are prepared to offer"	"We offer"
"We have to acknowledge receipt of"	"We have received"
"Communicate"	"Write" or "Send"
"We are in agreement"	"We agree"
"Wholly unfounded"	"Not true"
"We are the recipients of"	"We have"
"It will be our earnest endeavour"	"We shall try"
"Furnish all necessary particulars"	"Give details"
"Please be good enough to advise us"	"Please tell us"
"We confirm telephonic conversation with regard to the delay"	"We confirm telephone conversation about the delay"
"He was made the recipient of a special bonus by the company"	"The company gave him a special bonus"
"Awaiting your detailed instructions as to how you wish the goods to be shipped, and assuring you of our best attention at all times"	"As soon as we hear from you we shall ship the goods"
"Terminate"	"End"

Do not say	*Say instead*
"Utilize"	"Use"
"Acquaint"	"Tell"
"Assist"	"Help"
"Despatch"	"Send"
"Peruse"	"Read"
"Proceed"	"Go"
"Request"	"Ask"

Perhaps the best example of precise English used to give a perfectly clear instruction is to be found in the letter of David to Job, 2 Samuel ii, 14–15: "Set ye Uriah in the forefront of the hottest battle, and retire ye from him that he may be smitten and die."

Procedures when Writing

The following brief rules might suggest helpful procedures in writing—

1. WRITING

(*a*) Use short sentences—rarely allowing them to exceed about twenty words in length;

(*b*) choose sentence structures that require only simple punctuation;

(*c*) prefer the active voice of verbs;

(*d*) insert connectives and other reference words to ensure relationships;

(*e*) correct weak or vague references of pronouns to their antecedents;

(*f*) convert a loose compound sentence into a complex sentence with a subordinate clause.

2. CLARITY

Revise sentences and paragraphs with special attention to clarity. There should be only one possible meaning, and this should be easily understood by the reader. Find the word or phrase to convey your idea in the briefest possible way.

3. CONCISENESS

As a rule, the first draft of a circular letter, if one goes out at all, should be longer and more complete than the copy that will eventually be sent. Better results are usually obtained by condensing a long letter than by expanding a short one. In shortening a letter, condense or eliminate the parts which are least needed for clearness of presentation. Strike out all unnecessary words (especially adjectives and adverbs); replace a phrase with a word; eliminate repetition of an idea. In judging, put yourself in the place of the reader. It may take moral courage to "blue pencil" choice phrases, sentences or paragraphs, but the results may well justify the effect.

Dictating a Letter

Writing a letter is talking across distance by means of written words. It will be much better if a would-be writer, when initiating or replying to a substantial letter, *prepared* to dictate his letters and so avoid ruffling the feelings of his secretary. A useful means of preparation, as in public speaking, is to use postcards, on which are written assertions which the letter is intended to contain. It will be inadequate if the cards contain words which serve to remind the writer of what he wishes to say. It is important that *assertions* be used instead.

The person dictating the letter will then speak from these cards, and is likely to do so with far greater effectiveness than he might otherwise do. In this way a letter will be dictated without likely muddling or "er-umming." Muddles only lead to waste of time and misunderstandings. If there is no tidy mind beforehand it cannot be expected that a letter will be helpful.

Plain English

Remember that the average person receiving a letter is someone who likes plain English. He wants the gist of the correspondence quickly, and does not want essays and tracts. Long-winded and ponderous language is likely to be tiresome to him.

In a letter to the *Daily Telegraph*, a correspondent said: "Let us suppose one of the greatest sentences ever uttered by Mr. Churchill had been in long and not the short words he advocates. Let us imagine, for instance, that instead of, 'I can offer you only blood, sweat and tears,' he had said: 'The prospect whose imminence I have to communicate to you is characterized exclusively by features sanguinary, laborious and lachrymose.' Surely the result on morale would have been calamitous."

In conclusion, as a summing-up of some of the elements of letter-writing referred to, a further quotation might be helpful. The poet, William Cowper, spoke his mind on this subject. He aimed to write sensibly only his uppermost thoughts. The following letter he wrote in 1780: "You like to hear from me: this is a very good reason why I should write. But I have nothing to say; this seems equally a good reason why I should not. Yet, if you had alighted from your horse at our door this morning, and at this present writing, being five o'clock in the afternoon, had found occasion to say to me, 'Mr. Cowper, you have not spoken since I came in; have you resolved never to speak again?' it would be but a poor reply, if, in answer to the summons, I should plead inability as my best and only excuse. And this, by the way, suggests to me a seasonable piece of instruction, and reminds me of what I am very apt to forget, when I have any epistolary business in hand, that a letter may be written upon anything or nothing, just as anything or nothing happens to occur. A man that has a journey before him, twenty miles in length, which he is to perform on foot, will not hesitate and doubt whether he shall set out or not, because he does not readily conceive how he shall ever reach the end of it; for he knows, that by the simple operation of moving one foot forward first, and then the other, he shall be sure to accomplish it.

"So it is in the present case, and so it is in every similar case. A letter is written as a conversation is maintained, or a journey performed; not by preconcerted, or premediated means, a new contrivance, or an invention never heard of before, but merely by maintaining a progress, and resolving as a postilion does, having once set out, never to stop till we reach the appointed end."

12 Presenting Technical Information

A Chapter on Reporting

J. M. Barrie once said: "The man of science appears to be the only man who has something to say just now, and the only man who doesn't know how to say it." It will be wise to look at the purpose and meaning of a specialist's writing and its place in an industrial setting.

Professor R. O. Kapp has written a book on *The Presentation of Technical Information*. This book, although it is small, is outstanding on the difficulty of report writing. Indeed, along with Nelson's book, it can be said to be one of the best treatises existing.

Writing is an art calling for care and method. It has been said (the author is not known): "The man of science makes a fetish of efficiency, yet he shows little regard for the effective use of one of his most important tools—the pen. He believes devoutly in accuracy, yet employs this instrument as carelessly as a small boy employs a gun."

Language is not an affair of temperament and therefore a matter of personal choice. Certainly it is not a matter of temperament when we are trying to communicate information. We bungle language deplorably, as unedifying examples of poor English will show. Technical writing is the *exact* expression of special knowledge. Through spacing and layout, prominence should be given to certain topics to enable a reader to distinguish easily what is worth knowing and what must be remembered.

There is necessarily, without adding to ambiguity, a high level of abstraction in the language of science. It possesses concepts and ideas which are bound to have more than local applicability. Technical language is too often general and therefore too often abstract.

Writing for the Reader

The writer, however, must state for the reader's benefit precisely what the crux of a situation is. The heart of the problem must be stated, and not assumed. He must make clear what observations are pertinent and why.

Knowledge comes in *patterns* and it is important for a writer to explain to a reader just what the writer's patterns of thinking are. It is not merely a matter of convention, but obviously of sheer practical importance, that the answers to questions involving technical operations should so be presented as to be understood by the people who have to use the answers. Only the technical or scientific man can answer questions thoroughly, in view of his technical knowledge.

Management may, nevertheless, not understand him, not through stupidity but because the writer has not effectively explained his own thinking or his own answers. The more information management can get the better off management is.

Writing in Industry

We are concerned with the ability to write tersely, to state facts plainly and to convey information intelligibly. In technical operations the scientist may be concerned with difficult matter, but when writing a report it is meant to be read by one's fellows.

A capable writer will evoke the sympathy of his readers, and so should write within their understanding and experience. Herbert Spencer speaks of discipline and of the creation of intellectual sympathy when writing, and asks for such an insight into another's intellectual state as is needed rightly to adjust the sequence of ideas to be connected.

One should therefore spare the reader—

1. doubt as to the meaning of what is written;
2. perplexity caused by clumsiness of style;
3. annoyance at unnecessarily technical terms;
4. weariness owing to verbosity.

The reader of a report would probably have no difficulty when words referred to material elements, but he would have difficulty where the words referred to *concepts* or relationships and processes. These concepts may be described in language and even identified by words, but learning them takes experience, time and thought.

The language of the writer must not create the least trouble to the reader. To quote Herbert Spencer: "The most effective modes of expression are those which absorb the smallest amount of the recipient's attention interpreting the symbols of thought, leaving the greatest amount of time for the thought itself." This means that economy of mental effort should be asked for by the writer from his reader. Language should be an *effective* medium for the transmission of thought, and the reader must not have to probe the writing to discover its meaning.

T. H. Huxley once said that, if a man really knows his subject, "he will be able to speak of it in an easy language and with the completeness of conviction with which he talks of an everyday matter. If he does not he will be afraid to wander beyond the limits of technical phraseology which he has got up." Even if this comment is a slight exaggeration, the fundamental truths of any science can be told in the simplest writing without loss of accuracy. Indeed, the ability to explain technical matters to the unlearned is a test of one's own thoroughness of understanding.

Writing must be done carefully if a technical description is to hold interest. "It is not enough to use language that *may* be understood, it is necessary to use language that *must* be understood." We have not only to *express* ideas but to *communicate* them. "Three classes of men do not tell the truth except by mistake: (1) those who do not know it; (2) those who wish not to tell it; (3) those who do not know how to tell it."

Precision

There are certain things one can say precisely, and there are other things it is not possible to be precise about. For example, it would be impossible to describe the difference between the smell of boiling cabbage and the smell of a rose precisely. If a person is capable of being precise, then he should be, and there is no excuse for him if he is not. % is a precise sign, and therefore should not be used otherwise. There is simply no excuse for the writer of a report to speak of mixing 75% sand with 25% lime. What he really means is three parts sand and one part lime. Similarly, words like "considerable" and "large" are unhelpful to the reader.

One of the greatest enemies to precision in technical writing is the continuous use of the abstract instead of the concrete noun. Quiller-Couch, at the turn of the century, said that the mark of the virile writer lay in the use of the concrete noun and the active verb. It is hard to understand why this sage advice has remained unheeded. People speak of "a conveyance" when they mean "to convey"; or "success in avoiding" when they mean "will avoid."

Another enemy to precision is the constant use of the passive voice. When there is a description of an experiment the writer will say "a crucible was taken," "it is submitted," and so forth, until no one appears to be doing anything, things only seem to happen. The passive voice has been often used in this book, but there are still qualms about offending long-standing if stupid conventions.

Not only should a writer know what his words denote, but he should know how to build his sentences. He has, of course, to be careful in selecting his words, but he must also contruct his sentences properly. This is said not simply from the point of view of the grammarian or teacher, but from the point of view of the manager; the latter is a busy reader, and is affected by such care.

Reporting is part of any communication system, and the technician or technologist is part of the industrial organization. He is not an isolated worker writing out his findings. If one were a scientist only, the matter would be much simpler. The graduate, however, is not merely a scientist, but a scientist in industry. He should know who his reader is and what he wants to understand. One would issue a caveat, trite though it is, to him: "Think before you write." He should clarify for himself which idea goes first *from the reader's point of view*, which idea can be left out, and which idea needs explanations. He must understand not only his own special field of activity, but also the general context in which he operates, namely the business context. He is connected with that context for speaking and writing.

A writer is not communicating merely when he writes, but when he is read and understood. Report writing is, after all, a co-operative effort. Each person within an organization must know what the other is doing. The scientist or technician is conveying information in a business context. His report is an essential part of his job—in fact a culmination of his job. He must know, therefore, what is done with the report and how it fits into the total picture. If he does not know this, then we can only speak of faulty management and say that communication is bad.

Asking for a Report

A report is asked for, not volunteered. The person asking for it must be quite definite in his request. What has been said about the need for precision on the part of the writer is equally applicable to the person calling for the report. Once again, the best way of asking for a report is to ask a question to which the report will be an answer. The writer is then far more likely to write pertinently and helpfully.

Types of Report

We should distinguish between three types of report: the expository report which is either descriptive or narrative; the interpretative report, which is an interpretation of facts or ideas; the argumentative report, which is probably the most difficult to write.

The *narrative* exposition, which might be an account of a process of manufacturing or operations, is thoroughly concrete and even chronological. It should *move*, as any narration should do. The reader must know exactly where he is going and why. An account is of little help unless it has some practical purpose behind it. A narrative exposition should begin with a summary of what has gone before, as this will help the reader in his effort to grasp further details with more understanding and interest.

The *interpretative* report gives meanings to facts and concepts. One of the assumptions we often make, but are not entitled to make, is that people will interpret a thing as we do. This is not true, for experience gives meanings both to facts and to ideas. Because we have a particular interest, meanings may be obvious to us, but not obvious to the person without that interest.

The *argumentative* report is one that will be looked at more closely in Chapter 16. The main thing one should stress here is the need to distinguish carefully between fact and comment on it. Because in argument he who asserts must prove, it must be quite clear to the reader *what assertions the writer of the report is making*. The reader must not have to sort out what is an actual assertion and what is an expression of opinion. In the argumentative report, it must be quite clear precisely how the writer is arriving at his main propositions.

Reports in Practice

Reports are a practical operational job providing the setting for sound policies and sound decisions. Consequently the emphasis in the report has to be on facts and explanations, rather than on opinions. That is why the style has to be business-like, with little emotional effects and no exaggeration.

A report should also have a clear distinction in it between "facts" that are hearsay and facts that are observed. Very often a writer will put something down that he has been told about or read about, without making his reference clear. It is not always possible to assess whether the writer has observed the thing for himself or has been told about it.

There should be, as in meetings, numbers of intermediate summaries. For example, one might say: "Thus far so-and-so has been said; from here let us go on to prove such-and-such."

The Value of a Synopsis

Every major report should be preceded by a synopsis; a shorter statement could be sent to all the people concerned, and those then wanting to read the full report will ask for it and probably get better value out of it.

Organizing a Report

We may organize our report in one way for a particular individual and in another way for another individual. Two such ways of setting out a report are the inductive way and the deductive way. By the *inductive* way is meant that the report starts with an introduction, which states the problem, defining the subject and the scope and purpose of the problem; then comes the body of the report; then there is the conclusion, and finally the recommendations based on the conclusion. The *deductive* report, on the other hand, aims to present the conclusions first, and the data which produced them secondly. The report starts with a summary followed by an introduction and the conclusions and finally the text is given.

When, as with some writers, mention is made of the "logic of layout," the question arises of the meaning we are to attach to the word "logic." The meaning becomes clear when one appreciates that within industry reports are written to be acted upon; what is and what is not "logic in the layout of the report" will depend largely upon the needs and capacity of the reader; there must obviously be an orderly sequence of ideas which can be easily perceived by the reader and which will carry him along with the minimum of distraction. Thus, by being "logical" we mean giving *direction* to our thought and giving direction to our expression in such a manner that that direction will be easily perceived.

Suggested Scheme of Division in the Layout of a Report

A technical report is generally a combination of a report of facts and an interpretation of facts. A recommendation may be expressed or implied—involving the added element of persuasion.

No particular method will suit all reports. The method of writing depends on many conditions: e.g. the nature of the subject, the purpose of the report, the characteristics of the writer, the interests of the readers. But there must be some plan of composition, and that plan must be very clear to the reader. A report is intended to be studied and used as a reference; it is not intended merely to be read.

As has been suggested, each part of a report should provide answers to the following questions—

1. *Why* has the work been done?
2. *What* work was done?
3. What were the *results*?
4. What do the results *mean*?
5. What *action* do these results suggest?

The report should contain an *introduction* stating—

1. nature of the problem; its condition at the beginning of the inquiry; background information;

2. purpose, scope and method of the inquiry;

3. most significant outcome of the inquiry: the state of the problem at the end of the inquiry.

The introduction sets out the purpose of the work, the problem to be solved, and the questions to be answered. Sometimes the mere statement of the problem is not sufficient. The reader may not possess enough information to realize the significance of the problem. A background of knowledge about the problem will help. This knowledge may be of the kind that is known to everyone working in the field, or it may be the result of some recent work reported under another inquiry.

PROCEDURE AND RESULTS

Give a brief description of what was done, how it was done and what results were obtained; it is better to give only a brief survey at this stage, and to leave the details of the experiment for a supplementary experimental section.

This division should include only a brief description of the work done. The results should be limited to the more important data. Only enough material should be included to enable the reader to understand the writer's conclusions and recommendations.

CONCLUSIONS AND RECOMMENDATIONS

Significance of results, conclusions to be drawn from them and recommendations.

This division contains a short statement of the conclusions reached, a condensed discussion of the evidence leading to these conclusions, and recommendations. The conclusions are the answers to the questions raised at the beginning of the report.

DISCUSSION OF RESULTS

1. Main principles (casual relations or generalizations that are shown by the results);

2. evidence for each of the main conclusions;

3. exceptions and opposing theories, with explanations of them;

4. comparison of the writer's results and interpretations with those of other workers.

The writer should emphasize conclusions that modify in a significant way any principle that has secured general acceptance. To prevent misunderstanding, it is necessary to define as clearly as possible the conditions to which the writer's conclusions apply. A conclusion should always be stated in such a way as to indicate its range of validity. Confusion often results from failure to define adequately all influential experimental details.

EXPERIMENTAL PARAGRAPHS

Apparatus, evaluation and discussion of results, any special procedures, graphs and tables.

The final order of presentation is not necessarily the order in which the report is *written.*

The experimental paragraphs contain an account of the work in such detail that it can be checked or repeated at a later date. They should include a description of the experiment and methods used, a description of any analyses made or of any experiment held, and a detailed discussion of any experimental facts which have a bearing on the conclusion or recommendations.

DIGESTS

Digests, which are often typed separately and circulated to executives and certain other employees, are intended to keep those people informed who do not have time to read the whole report. Compactness and clarity are therefore essential. Digests should even be understood by persons to whom the technical aspects of the inquiry are not known.

As the whole report is not always circulated with the digest, it is important for the digest to tell a complete story—

1. An introduction, which relates the present report to previous reports;

2. an abstract of the present report;

3. an outline of work planned for the future.

S. F. Trelease, in *How to Write Scientific and Technical Papers* has this advice to offer—

Use of Tenses

1. *Experimental Facts.* The experimental facts should be given in the *past tense.*

(For example: The plants *grew* better in A than in B; the dry weight *was* greater in A than in B.)

2. *Presentation.* The remarks about the presentation of data should be mainly in the *present tense.*

(For example: Diagrams showing yields *are* shown in Figure 3. The second column of Table 2 *represents* the dry weight of tops.)

3. *Discussion of Results.* Discussions of results may be in both the *past* and *present* tenses, swinging back and forth from the experimental facts to the presentation.

(For example: The highest dry weight *is* shown for culture A, which *received* the greatest amount of the ammonium salt. This may mean that the amount of nitrogen added *was* the determining condition for these experiments.)

4. *Specific Conclusions.* Specific conclusions and deductions should be stated in the *past tense,* because this always emphasizes the special conditions of the particular experiments and avoids confusing special conclusions with general ones.

(For example: Rice *grew* better, under the other conditions of these tests, when ammonium sulphate *was* added to the soil. Do not say: Rice *grows* better when ammonium sulphate *is* added to the soil.)

5. *General Truths.* When a general truth is mentioned, it should, of course, be stated in the *present tense.* Logically, a general truth is without time distinction. (For example, one may say: "Many years ago, scientists were convinced

that malaria *is* caused by a germ carried by a certain species of mosquito.") General conclusions, well-established principles of mathematics, physics and chemistry, should be put in the *present tense*.

Check List on some Common Errors in Writing

1. *Inaccuracy*
(a) Mis-statement or exaggeration of fact.
(b) Misrepresentation through omission of fact.
(c) Errors in data, terms, citations.
(d) Conclusions based on faulty or insufficient evidence.
(e) Unreliable mathematical treatment.
(f) Failure to distinguish between fact and opinion.
(g) Contradictions and inconsistencies.

2. *Inadequate Presentation*
(a) Omission of important topics.
(b) Faulty order of sections or of paragraphs.
(c) Inclusion of material in wrong section or paragraph.
(d) Incomplete development of a topic.
(e) Failure to begin a section or a paragraph with a topic sentence.
(f) Weak beginning of a section or a paragraph.
(g) Inclusion of irrelevant or tedious details.
(h) Passages that are dull or hard to read.
(i) Failure to distinguish between the new and the well known.
(j) Inadequate emphasis of interpretation and conclusions.

3. *Diction and Style*
(a) Long sentences (more than two or three typewritten lines) and complicated grammar.
(b) Weak sentence beginnings—a string of weak or meaningless words.

(*c*) Lack of clarity—a sentence that requires re-reading to get the meaning.

(*d*) Long, complicated paragraphs.

(*e*) Wordiness and padding—failure to come directly to the point.

(*f*) General words rather than definite words.

(*g*) Dull, weak, or awkward expressions.

(*h*) Unnecessary repetition of the same word or the same sentence structure.

(*i*) Omission of relation words, especially in short sentences.

(*j*) Unnecessarily technical language or too many strange words in a single sentence.

13 Becoming Aware of Attitudes Towards an Actual or Proposed Job

A Chapter on Interviewing

"INTERVIEWING" has been much written about in human relations. More books and articles have been written about the psychology of the interview than there are grains in the proverbial sand. Some of these books and articles have given sage counsel, and probably the most helpful is *The Psychology of the Interview* by R. C. Oldfield. It is not our purpose to duplicate the good advice given. It may be useful, however, to look at interviewing briefly against the background of communication in general.

There are quite definite main types of interview—

1. The interview held as supplementary to a written examination; the purpose is to find out if the candidate has a full understanding of his subject.

2. The interview for a job requiring qualifications other than purely technical. Those doing the interviewing are frequently vague about their aim, so that candidates for the one position are interviewed from very different points of view.

3. The "non-directive" interview, as opposed to the "directive" interview which rests on the framing of specific questions to obtain specific answers. The "non-directive" interview is one in which the interviewer listens rather than speaks, never gives advice, remains morally neutral, and treats as confidential everything that he hears.

C. W. Valentine in *Psychology and its Bearing on Education*, speaks of an experiment in which sixteen university graduates were interviewed "by two boards of four or five eminent persons, including two university professors, a chief inspector, and a headmaster of a public school. Each board interviewed each of sixteen graduates for not less than a quarter of an hour and not more than half an hour. They were to test their alertness, intelligence and intellectual outlook with a view to deciding the value of the candidates' 'personality' for the Home Civil Service. To give a strong motive to candidates to do their best a prize of £100 was offered for the one selected . . .. When the orders of merit for the two boards were compared it was found that the man placed first by board A was put thirteenth by board B, while the man placed first by board B was eleventh with board A. If there had been six vacancies to be filled, five out of the six recommended by board A would have been different men from those recommended by B. The correlation between marks given by the two boards was only 0·41."

Prejudice

It would naturally be a very bad thing indeed if an interviewer were at all prejudiced. If he were, he would be likely to develop, and exhibit, attitudes which would either arouse the fear or anger, or thoroughly upset, the interviewee. This would be in addition to any prejudiced assessment. Bias might also indicate that a need different from that of good selection is being satisfied by the interview.

In interviewing in general the interviewer seeks to get from the candidate in question quite definite information that can be checked; he notes his appearance, voice and manner; and is helped by the general impression that the candidate's personality makes on him. Not only what a candidate says, but the manner in which he says it, may betray the candidate's personality. The interviewer should have a good idea of what he wants to find out, and have in his mind the relevant questions that he should ask. If, in the course of the interview, tests can be given, this may throw a great deal of light on the candidate's temperamental qualities. With adults, however, this is not really possible. Questioning plays a great part in interviewing, and it would be better and easier to begin with questions that concern matters of fact.

Questions Asked by the Interviewer

There are six or seven possible questions which an interviewer might ask—

1. The names of past employers:
    (*a*) How did the interviewee get the position?
    (*b*) What did he do?
    (*c*) Why did he leave?
2. How did previous employers treat him?
3. What experience, if any, of value did he get from each job?
4. Did he achieve work of such quality that his employer would be glad to recommend him?
5. Was he ever criticized for the amount of work he did? He should then be required to give examples of mistakes or possible failures.
6. He should be asked to give examples of success in his experience, particularly in handling people.
7. What kind of work did he enjoy most and appear to progress well in?

If the interview is intended to help an employee, one may assume that a number of interviews would be required. Such interviews should have a time limit of about three-quarters of an hour. The employee should be made to feel that the period given to the interview is his if he wishes to use it. A pre-arranged time for ending any interview makes it unnecessary for the interviewer to find an excuse for breaking off a long session, and it also avoids making the employee feel that he may have "overstayed his welcome."

At a large London store, the personnel manageress has set aside a time each day, from 4 o'clock onwards, when she would be prepared to see any member of staff who might go to her for advice. Members of staff thus know that a definite period of time is available to them.

Dr. May Smith, in *An Introduction to Industrial Psychology*, said: "Definite rules are not likely to help, since most people have to evolve their own methods, but in the light of a little knowledge of the errors made some general points of view are given—

1. "The ordinary rules of courtesy that normally obtain between human beings should always be observed. The person in high authority who snaps at the junior he is interviewing as a beginning is illustrating what not to do, but unfortunately he is setting a pattern that might be followed by the chosen candidate when he is in authority.

2. "A casual manner affected in a misplaced attempt to be informal often defeats its object. The candidate should be able to feel that his interviewer is interested in him.

3. "The interviewer should listen as much as possible, only giving his own views if it is necessary to encourage the candidate.

"As the interview progresses, a general impression of the candidate will be forming, which will gradually receive definition. The form this impression takes varies from person to person according to his own make-up. The good visualizer may be seeing the candidate in his mind's eye in the position he is seeking, picturing him getting on, or not."

Grievances

When an employee comes to one's office with grievances, listening and sympathy are the main requirements. One should listen to him and let him unburden himself, when he will perhaps see his own answers. This is by far the better way. But listening to grievances is recognizing them as symptoms and identifying the meaning of them.

When employment has terminated, it may be advisable to find out exactly why an employee is leaving. An interviewer might be serving a useful purpose if—

1. He finds out why the employee wishes to go. The cause may be corrected and the employee may be induced to stay.

2. He uses reason, not pressure, in inducing the employee to change his mind. This may require a diplomatic approach to a director.

3. If the employee speaks about leaving, the interviewer should show how it may still be possible to keep the job and yet retain prestige.

It is obvious that an interviewee should be made to feel at ease. This can be achieved by not conducting the interview in one's own office. The owner of the office will be familiar with the placing of all his furniture and other possessions and feel consequently at ease, but the interviewee will be strange to the environment and so probably less comfortable mentally. The interviewee is in the position of being either a newcomer, a person moving from one department to another, or an employee in trouble. It will not, therefore, be easy for him to act with entire self-possession.

Beginning of an Interview

The way the beginning of an interview is conducted is most important. It is necessary to obtain a good conversational topic, one which will be easy to the interviewee and probably familiar to him. *Accord* has to be created right at the beginning. When people start talking on matters of common interest, they are more likely to feel on an equal footing. People speak frankly when the situation is permissive, and the interviewer appears to be understanding.

Co-operative behaviour occurs when there is a common interest. It should not be difficult to find an interest that both people share. The applicant, of course, wants to be in a job that will make use of his special aptitudes and training;

this is what a company may want. If a common interest is established, the applicant will express preferences and so disclose his true feelings and aspirations.

The relationship between interviewee and interviewer should be helpful rather than based on apparent judgement.

Questions

It has been argued that questions should not be too specific, and thereby greater opportunity given for general discourse upon a topic. This is probably true, but no question should be so diffuse that the interviewee is hard put to it to gather its true sense.

Since each interview has a special purpose, questions may be needed to control the topic of discussion. In counselling one may not wish to channel discussion, and may deliberately ask wide questions. A question can nevertheless direct the discussion and still be able to explore a person's feelings. This latter type of question may specify the general topic, yet allow the interviewee a great deal of freedom.

To the extent that the employee interviewed can choose from a number of possible reactions to a question, the interview is centred in the interviewee and an interest in him and his feelings is indicated. Certainly the specific question may be asked, as confidence and trust grow, in a well-conducted interview; for as we have already observed, a good question stimulates original thinking.

The attitudes, maintains Oldfield, should be closely *perceived* and not merely be the result of *inference*. The interviewer must first perceive what the attitudes are and then perhaps form possible judgements on them at a later time.

Attitudes

The term "attitude" is stressed by Oldfield, who maintained that the aim of a successful interview is to secure a display of attitudes. Agreement with him is possible, more particularly as he relates the word to *activity*. An attitude is a reaction based on experience. It indicates not merely what a person thinks, but what he is likely *to do* in a given situation.

Psychologically, an attitude is a kind of predisposition to form certain opinions. Opinions based on facts offer no problem, for opinions change immediately conditions are altered; but when opinions are based on attitudes they are a particular problem, as unfavourable attitudes can continue even after the conditions have been changed.

The attitude should be thought of as the general background of feeling against which factual events are examined. Disagreement over the nature of given facts may be because the prevailing attitude influences the way the facts are experienced. Indeed, attitudes often determine the meanings given to facts as to words. N. R. F. Maier, in *Psychology in Industry*, has this to say: "Attitudes usually are associated with the likes and dislikes and consequently have an emotional content. Thus any condition which influences men is likely to influence certain attitudes. Our moods are temporary predispositions towards having certain emotional reactions. As a consequence, it is to be expected that a mood will influence our attitudes. . . . Because opinions and emotional reactions are often closely associated, mood and attitude are frequently difficult to differentiate. . . . We often think that our opinions are based solely on our thinking or reasoning. The study of attitudes requires an alteration of this belief. Man is not so rational a being as he would like to think himself. Rather, he holds opinions which are largely influenced by attitude and then uses his reason to defend his opinions. Such rationalization is a common form of mental activity. We all know that man may fail to change his opinion, even though we refute every one of the points he has used to support his position. He merely develops another set of reasons. Our efforts have changed only his justifications and defences.

11—(B.648)

"This does not mean that reason never influences opinion. It is our purpose to point out that attitude is the more important factor, and that it influences, not a large number of people in all their opinions, but all the people in a great many of their opinions. On some subjects practically all people are reasonable, and on others practically all have an emotional bias."

14 Giving Authority to Others

A Chapter on Delegation

In our attempts to deal with this controversial subject, it is to advantage that we have already had the opportunity of expressing views on problems of communication in management. It is well to emphasize that effective delegation is part of communication activity, with recognition of all the practices and conventions that effective communication demands. Reference should be made to the first two chapters.

When a subject of this kind is examined, it is easy—and sometimes just—to question how far the practices of higher management conform to ideal conceptions. The main purpose, however, is to re-examine practices in the light of ideal thinking. The main purpose of this chapter, therefore, will be to present points of view and to raise questions which may provoke self-searching and a review of present departmental administration.

When the word "manager" is used it shall mean anyone who is responsible for the activity of others.

The verb "delegate" in its original connotation—and we know that connotations change in different contexts—means to appoint a representative or ambassador. In this sense members of departments and sections can be said to be delegates of firms in relation to the public throughout each working day.

"Delegate" also literally means to entrust a group of people to the care and management of someone else. We should examine how far we effectively commit our staffs to the care and management of others, how far we make it possible for this care and management to be effective, and so how far we are aware of the twin concepts of responsibility and authority and the connexions between them.

Both these senses of "delegation" must be borne in mind when we discuss it: we cannot deal with it merely in terms of apportioning responsibility, or by making obvious statements about authority being commensurate with responsibility. The word "delegate" has developed far wider connotations than superficially appear.

We must therefore—

1. consider duties in regard to—

(*a*) employees in relation to supervisors or managers;

(*b*) managers or supervisors in relation to workers; and

(*c*) all persons in relation to their department as a total unit. A working group has a personality of its own, just as do the individuals who constitute the group. This group personality may or may not be worthily representative of the total organization-personality to which a firm aspires;

2. consider duties in regard to problems of control.

These considerations may be discussed under two heads of argument, which we shall attempt to outline in this chapter—

A. Delegation in the wider sense of establishing all members of staff of departments as worthy representatives and ambassadors of the firm.

B. Delegation in the more precise sense of clearly defining and granting areas of responsibility and authority for efficient overall performance.

Establishing Worthy Representatives

Delegation in the wider sense is achieved through the effectiveness of formal *and informal* relations with members of departments. Delegation in the more precise sense is achieved through a proper assessment of the meaning of "controlling" a department and an accurate delineation of the functions of those who supervise under management.

When "responsibility" is used within the context of this chapter it is thought of as a moral attribute. It implies fulfilment of a task, a duty or an obligation, according to orders given. Authority is commonly delegated only to persons of proved responsibility.

Unless relations are good, no delegation of responsibility, however emphatic and authoritative it may be, will release the physical and mental energy that distinguishes effective representation from bad.

Good relations, as we know, within a working unit do not result from a mere declaration of responsibilities, however clear these may be. Of course, clarity in definition of responsibilities is necessary: this is the first requisite. Each head of a department should accept his obligation to prepare proper job descriptions for every employee. This job description must state not merely the tasks to be performed, but even the personal qualities, behaviour and attitudes that might control the performance. This is said, although one recognizes that telling a person *how* to do a thing may limit delegation. Indeed, without this requisite, true delegation has not even begun; without it, reprimand and criticism cease to have meaning or value.

The first manifestation of well-delegated responsibility, then, down to the lowest levels, is a full job description of operations and expected standards of performance. Subsequent training courses cannot wholly compensate for any failure to do this on the part of any executive.

Clear declarations of responsibility, to repeat, are in themselves not sufficient. If delegation—in this sense of creating worthy representation in the performance of the policy and practices of a closely-knit department—is to be really effective, we must not only assign responsibilities but create an atmosphere or working climate in which they can be willingly and energetically carried out. In other words, with the creation of responsibility goes the creation of morale.

MORALE

The American writer, H. A. Overstreet, in *The Mind Goes Forth*, has said: "Morale is a state of faith. In military, political or industrial affairs it is essentially faith—in the organization, in its leadership, in its objectives, in the achievement of these objectives. Morale is personal in origin, for, as Napoleon said; 'There is no such thing as a good regiment or bad regiment, but there is such a thing as a good or bad colonel.' Organization morale thus operates from the top down. Only enlightened leadership in action can produce the *esprit de corps* that distinguishes the alert, aggressive, continuously advancing army, party, or business institution."

Morale results from making proper demands upon people, "demands which enable them to win the psychological rewards of achievement. It connotes energy, eagerness, teamwork, success; lack of morale is marked by confusion, apathy, muddling and failure . . . *Leadership* is the art of getting people in the right frame of mind to do their best. Morale is that quality of physical, mental and spiritual fitness that demands the release in action against the required objective."

DELEGATING A SENSE OF RESPONSIBILITY

Our obligation, then, in the delegation of a sense of responsibility is—

1. to maintain morale where it exists to a satisfactory degree;
2. to increase or intensify it where it exists, but may be improved;
3. to create it where it is lacking;
4. to change negative morale attitudes into those which are positive.

Morale cannot be forced. It must be induced. Unjust or indifferent treatment, unwarranted severity, and many other acts on the part of supervision inevitably affect the way employees feel and the loyalty they show (in performance as well as in attitude) towards their firm. Prompt handling of complaints, dealing fairly with all employees, carefully interpreting and explaining any management regulations which may be causing unrest, explaining the causes for policy or action, and other similar ways of dealing with people will remove most of the causes of lost morale. The right mental attitude of any employee depends on whether he is interested in his job, satisfied with it, and feels that his chief is an able, trustworthy leader whom it is worthwhile to rally around and follow.

All this demands, of course, that integrity should be unmistakable and that our own enthusiasm should be imparted to others. But it also demands that our action be visibly *decisive*, and that it be clear to all that we maintain the highest degree of co-ordination of effort at all levels of authority and at all degrees of responsibility.

As was emphasized in discussing communication, successful co-ordination demands that there be a steady flow of essential and useful information at and between all levels. The unity that arises from active participation of all members of a department—through the possession of essential information—in the formulation of orders that involve them not only lessens the difficulties of co-ordination but makes possible an entire morale-building programme.

Within a short space one can say little more on this aspect of the problem of delegation—that is, on making the responsibilities of one's subordinates articulate in both the operational and personal sense, and on accepting one's own responsibilities to go beyond definition and *to create the feeling of unity in performance that results from effective morale.*

We must, however, appreciate that effective morale must be evidenced throughout successive executive ranks. If morale in supervision is low, anyone entrusted with a supervisory position will, apart from his own grievances, dampen the reactions of employees to the spirit of the enterprise and defeat the good work done by management. Nothing is more calculated to damage morale and so lessen the effectiveness of supervisors than a vague conception of accountability or authority.

It is, therefore, just here that we face the more precise meaning of "delegation" in the more obvious sense of easing a managerial and supervisory burden by the apportionment of duties with relevant authority. This involves us in brief reference to the concepts of control and accountability.

Responsibility and Authority

We are, then, now concerned with the relationship between employees and supervisors or managers.

What has been said about definition of responsibilities applies of course with particular significance for those who have supervisory or managerial duties. It is essential that they know precisely what primary activities they are expected to perform in regard to operational tasks and in regard to personnel. These activities are their contribution to the goal and objectives of the firm. But here we must cautiously distinguish between telling a person *what* to do, and telling him *how* to do it.

To the extent that we tell a person *how* to do a thing, to that extent do we really limit delegation. We necessarily place a restriction on initiative. In examining the art of delegation, therefore, we must consider the *restraints* that should be imposed when explaining responsibilities, as much as we should consider the *detailed* information that should accompany the delineation of responsibilities.

We must seek to develop confidence in members (particularly the more senior members) of staffs, and we must give them the *opportunity* to *merit* this confidence. This means giving them *scope for initiative* as well as scope for the exercise of authority necessary to execute their duties.

AUTHORITY

Just as we cannot conceive of authority without responsibility we cannot conceive of responsibility without authority.

There are many people with management or supervisory burdens who do not realize that delegation of authority, by easing the burden of management, makes for greater efficiency. There is in them an innate aversion to delegating authority. This may be because of a desire to hold all the authoritative strings out of a sense of self-importance.

Most likely it is because of fear—fear that they will be criticized if a subordinate lets them down. They therefore sacrifice a great deal of potential efficiency to selfishness, prejudice or fear. They blind themselves to recognition that the authority vested in a person must be *adequate* to the responsibility given.

This is foolish even from a selfish point of view. Delegation of duties, with appropriate authority, ought to free a departmental manager from many of his worries and ease many of his problems. It ought to enable him to devote more time and thought to planning, improvising, or expanding.

Elbourne in *Fundamentals of Industrial Administration* says: "Dissemination of leadership may best be effected by successive delegation . . . but though administration gains its greatest effectiveness by this means, comparatively few executives possess sufficient wisdom, perception, restraint and unselfishness to enable them to delegate sufficiently, satisfactorily and therefore successfully."

ACCOUNTABILITY

Regard must be had, further, to the principle of *accountability*. This must be clearly established. A person is responsible *for* something, and the necessary authority for achieving that something must be inherent in the position. But he is also responsible *to* someone for what he does. So that, as Colonel Urwick has said, "every individual is entitled to know two things—to whom he is responsible and for what, and how that immediate authority is linked up with the supreme authority which represents the purpose of the system of co-operation as a whole."

Not only must accountability be clear, but the accountability *periods* must be clear. That is, a person should know at what stated intervals of time he is to account for what he does. Unless this clarity is achieved, doubt and anxiety must inevitably result in the performance of duties which call for initiative, decisiveness and discretion.

CONTROL

Finally, let us look briefly at the principle of control. This has been defined as "the technique of setting plans in motion by the release of orders, and of observing, inspecting and recording progress in such a manner as to keep up continuous comparison between planned and actual results." More shortly, in the words of Henri Fayol, control is "the ensuring that all which occurs is in accordance with the rules established and the instructions issued."

Control is effective in proportion to the accuracy of observing every definite step towards achieving a common goal. This is where effective communication must be accepted as a primary duty at every level of authority and degree of responsibility. The necessary steps towards achieving a goal must be clearly known by all people (at however low a level) contributing towards these steps.

Plans, orders, instructions, and reports on progress should be clearly known, not only by those with executive tasks but over as wide an area of the working force as possible.

It is only through a clear insight into situations giving rise to activity that members of our staffs will give the fullest effect to and develop such capacities and intelligence as they might have. And it is only because of this insight that we can expect the loyalty and allegiance that not only constitute morale, but make control a comparatively supple, pliable mechanism. To the degree to which there are not these insights into plans, orders and progress reports at all levels—insights into "the rules established and the instructions issued"—to that degree control becomes a struggle and deteriorates if it does not collapse. At best it is control impaired and efficiency diminished.

Conclusion

This theme of *delegation* could be discoursed upon at great length. But with concentration much can be done to examine—and perhaps revise—our meanings of the term. An attempt has been made to suggest a few extensions in meaning that the term might imply. It is for the reader to supply the better answers in the light of his special experience in his own firm.

It is easy for a term, by constant use, to become stale and blunted by that very use, and so to lose the connotations it should fairly have. Let us open our minds to fresh explorations.

15 Enthusiasm

A Chapter on Producing the Enthusiastic Employee

THE affectation of cynicism, so often the first easy defence against ideas and points of view contrary to one's own ideas and practices, might well be encouraged by an apparent plea for "enthusiasm." Because this defence is so easy, and so often thoughtless, it is seldom impressive.

To be fair, however, to the would-be cynic, talk of "enthusiasm" might well be suspect. For is not the word itself an uncomfortable word? Its range of application in the hands of many tract writers, more particularly trans-atlantic apostles of western efficiency and "go-aheadness," is almost overwhelming. The meanings that emerge appear to be "passionate excitement in pursuit of an object," "ardent zeal," "heated imagination"—and, generally, excessively earnest and devoted attachment to a cause or object. These applications of the word "enthusiasm" suggest the predominance of the emotional over the intellectual powers.

In these senses the word has so many embarrassing, or even appalling, associations. It brings to mind the formidable door-to-door salesman lathered by his own energy and rapid talk in the sale of trifles; or the indefatigable organizer of games and social life aboard a ship, in relation to whom one is truly betwixt the devil and the deep blue sea; or the zealot of the great open air, banging us awake in the first light of a summer dawn for a swim, a shoot, a game with a ball, breathing life through his nostrils like some disordered soda-fountain; or the inveterate arranger of whist drives and rallies and social parties, or, last, the supervisor in a firm working himself like the door-to-door salesman into a lather of grim zeal, hustling a bewildered staff ignorant of the source or the object of either his grimness or his zeal. Enthusiasts most strange! The leaping lightning, Emerson would say, not to be measured by the horse-power of the understanding. A zealous man without imagination is a crank. A man in whom imagination gets the better of his judgement is also a crank.

But, of course, words mean what we want them to mean. Analysis of the word "enthusiasm" rids the word of these meanings. We shall not merely imply, within some simple cult of efficiency, that one stands like a greyhound in the slips straining upon the start. The term will be used operationally, within the general context of operations and expectations in which we work. The operations will of course vary.

"Enthusiasm" in a more sober context means maintaining in ourselves, and encouraging in others, attitudes of mind, forms of behaviour and qualities of concern and understanding that not only will keep our firms ahead in times of advancing competition, but will earn the continuing respect of our colleagues and subordinates alike. To be enthusiastic is to exert our capacities and our intelligence to the full, in application to our tasks and in our relations with others.

In regard to possible superiors we may perhaps, in our difficulties, be able to count on tolerance and the sympathetic indulgence of our weaknesses and mistakes, though this is not a wise reliance. But our subordinates will indulge neither our weaknesses nor our mistakes. Maintaining a constant mental vigilance, displaying constant self-control, constant maintenance of internal and external public relations at the highest levels of mutual respect—these are the hall-marks of the *enthusiastic* man or woman in the true performance of any supervisory or managerial responsibility.

Enthusiasm in this sense is like a fire. It needs both feeding and watching.

Exerting Intelligence and Capacity

One of the things most likely to happen, when undertaking any responsibility, is that we become habituated to certain routine ways of thought and behaviour. As affairs move reasonably satisfactorily, and there is no complaint or challenge to our performance, we assume that our existing knowledge is adequate and that our policy and standards of performance meet all requirements.

So we begin to act in a routine way with average accomplishment. We are no better and no worse than our predecessors. And we create successors whose knowledge and capacity for experience are perhaps even less than our own.

Exerting intelligence in any specialist job means *constantly furthering our knowledge*, re-examining our attitudes and assumptions, seeking out every opportunity for enhancing our judgement and skills. If we are truly responsive to the creative artist in each of us, we are never satisfied with our present understanding and the results it achieves.

But this responsibility for exertions extends beyond our relationship with ourselves: it extends to our relations with others—our colleagues, our subordinates.

To our possible superiors we have not merely the obligation to carry out assignments entrusted to us, and to improve upon performance as experience gathers, but to report back on discontents and prevailing attitudes of staff. This truism is no doubt accepted. As long as the attitudes are *manifest*, this latter task is simple enough. But to have the confidences of staff, sufficiently well to know their feelings otherwise unexpressed, is a consummation not so much devoutly to be *wished* as to be *striven* for—with all the exertion that responsible administration demands.

Teaching

The obligation to any superiors in the handling of staff extends even further. In their hands rests the future of a company, as well as its present success. Education for succession is not solely the function of formal staff training. Ultimately, line authority not only shares the responsibility, but has it in even greater measure. And the responsibility is realized, not only in the selection of probable successors, but in the overall *encouragement* of talent and interest latent in most people if we are diligent enough to seek them—or to inspire them.

So far from encouraging and developing the capacities of subordinates, however, without favour and bias, there are many managers and supervisors who stifle such initiative and enthusiasm as may initially exist. Often, as we have observed, people who have entered a firm with keenness, possessing wit and sensitive intelligence, have nevertheless degenerated over the years into utter mediocrities. For this tragedy—and it is no less than that—middle-management is mostly to blame. It fails to notice the alacrity of mind and attitude so necessary to sound leadership, in both the technical and the social sense.

Social Organization

However perfect, technically, an organization may be, however perfect its techniques and know-how, that organization will not flourish as effectively as it might unless the *social* organization is equally sound. This means more than creating an atmosphere of amiable relationships and benignity; it means tapping the large reserves of loyalty, cooperation and goodwill latent in practically every man; but this loyalty to be drawn out only by its being known and by the constant attentiveness and encouragement of those in charge.

To ask for this exertion in the tasks of supervision or management, is not to ask for too much. It is to ask of no greater exertion of intelligence and action than is rightfully demanded of any man or woman who accepts the tasks of supervision or management. Unless this obligation is known and accepted, there is a failure in responsibility to higher management, to the company, and not least, to the people who spend so great a part of their lives under our control.

It is so easy to place the blame on those we control. Our *egos*, indeed, demand that we do so. We condemn them as stupid, or stubborn or unco-operative or wilful. Our *egos* satisfied, and perhaps more determined than ever to display the authority we feel is being challenged, we make confusion worse confounded. Perhaps we continue but, our opportunities lost for expanding good-will, we lose to the company potential talents, energy, loyalty and strength.

Modern psychology and psychiatry now believe that where a person does not adjust himself well to the environment in which he lives and works, this is not due to some inner perversity or poison. It derives from some failure in his personal relations with others. A departmental head largely commands the success or the failure of the personal relations within it.

We work not merely in a context of events and happenings, but in an emotional context of inevitable conflicts and tensions. Only that supervisor or manager who has the fullest measure of enthusiasm—in the sense both of *dedication* and *understanding*—can meet this social challenge well and emerge as a figure deserving of both affection and respect.

Public Relations

No less than in the field of internal relations we at times exert ourselves in the field of public relations. Seldom is a supervisor or manager expected to be his own public relations officer. This is a fact which brings its own challenges, and demands its own qualities of personality and understanding. Once again, it is not sufficient to possess charm and friendliness, to be presentably dressed and well-mannered. Of course these things are important; they are the overt expression not only of personality, but of a sense of responsibility. But they are primarily the tools of the management profession; behind them must lie that perception and understanding of human motivation and behaviour which will enable a sensitive response to changing situations. To cope directly, or through our supervisors and staffs, with the men and women who pass our way is to be compelled to rely on more than intuition and native courtesy.

If we are interested in our jobs, then they must be explored theoretically as well as through daily experience. The especially appointed public relations officers of large concerns are noted for their enthusiasm both in activity and in *research*. Their understanding is developed through reading and conference, as well as through meeting the practical challenges of each day. Salesmanship, for example— whether of ideas or things—is a discipline worthy of study. As in all progessional and skilled jobs, the job is never sufficiently learnt, never sufficiently known. The educational process in all professions is a continuing one and calls not only for self-reliance, but self-criticism and humility.

The added responsibility of the supervisor or manager is that he must pass on an awareness of these disciplines to his subordinates, and counsel them in their acquisition.

The plea for enthusiasm is no hackneyed, sentimental appeal that springs merely from the normal preoccupation with the efficiency of "big business." It is a plea not only for vigour in action—it should be unnecessary to demand this— but for that exertion of will which will permit a continuing development of *understanding* which distinguishes the true leader.

In the execution of our responsibilities we can be equal to our performances in the past, or we can exceed them. We can barely justify expectations, or we can surpass them. The distinctive asset of enthusiasm—or the equally noticeable lack of it—will make the difference.

16 Argument

A Chapter on the Conventions of Sound Argument

In industry at least, it may not necessarily be convenient or helpful to be logical. To argue well, or effectively to disprove an argument, may collide painfully with a need to be tactful or silent.

In any event, formally correct logic may prove nothing or be unconvincing. For example, notices which point out the evils of smoking may be logical or systematic enough, but the inveterate smoker goes on smoking.

The fact remains that it may not be advisable to be logical. W. B. Yeats, the Irish poet and playwright, says in quite another context: "Argument, the moment victory is sought, becomes a clash of interests. One should not—above all in books which sign for immortality—argue at all if not ready to leave to another apparent victory. In daily life one becomes rude the moment one grudges to the clown his perpetual triumph." Although the context is different, what he says does apply to the industrial scene.

Experience does matter more than thoughtful conclusions. Real problems may be solved only in terms of long and practical experience, not in terms of intellectual theory; but if a person considers it expedient to be argumentative, he must argue well and be seen to argue well. After all, it must be remembered that respect (and *respect* does matter regarding authority) can only be earned; it cannot be demanded.

Definition

Obviously definition will play an important part in any argument. L. S. Stebbing, in her book *A Modern Introduction to Logic*, cites Plato, whose opinion was: "At present we are only agreed about the name. I dare say that we may both of us have the thing in our minds, but we ought always to come to an understanding about a thing in terms of a definition, and not merely about the name minus the definition."

Susan Stebbing put the matter this way: "Definition is an aid to clear thinking and, therefore, to the communication of thought. Sometimes when we are confronted with a problem, either theoretical or practical, or are trying—as we say —to 'think out' a subject, we find that we are thoroughly muddled. Our muddle may be due to the fact that either we do not see clearly what are the premises involved or we do not know exactly what it is we are thinking about. In the latter case we may succeed in thinking more clearly if we can define the words by which we are attempting to express our thought. We can define words only when we understand them. We understand a word when we know what it is to which the word refers or when we can use it significantly in combination with other words."

Gilbert Ryle says that logical thought is something dependent on "drills and skills." He is probably right. Reasoning does not come naturally to men; it is a technique that has to be learned.

Robert Thomson in *The Psychology of Thinking*, wrote: "The verb 'to think' has such a wide application that, in its most general use, we can never stop thinking throughout our waking moments, and even indulge in snatches of thought during sleep. Nevertheless we can distinguish several more particular meanings of the concept. What different kinds of activity does the notion of 'thinking' indicate according to conventional usage?" Perhaps the best answer to Robert Thomson's final question, certainly in this chapter where we are not concerned with the ambiguities of "thinking," would rest on four very clear types of the practical thinking process.

Sound Argument

Good argument requires the statement of both good and sufficient reasons. The reasons may be good ones, but insufficient for the proof necessary.

Any argument is based on an assertion, and there must be a good idea of what one wishes to prove. It is impossible, for example, to argue a single word or phrase; something quite definite must be asserted.

An argument is often confined to the truth or otherwise of an assertion. It seeks to let the single truth or untruth of what is argued influence action. It is therefore foolish for anyone to undertake to prove something true or untrue when he cannot do so from the very nature of the case before him. Sometimes a proposition is something on which evidence is just not available or an examination of all evidence is not possible.

Who Affirms Must Prove

The person making an assertion must prove it; on him rests the burden of proving his point. The burden does not immediately pass to one's opponent. It is common practice for a person to assert something and then say: "prove me wrong." This simply will not do. A person who makes a point has to establish its truth.

The burden of proof, however, often *shifts* as the argument proceeds. If a person making an assertion makes out a case that looks superficially good, then the burden of proof will shift to one's opponent. If a man is charged, for example, with libel, and a letter is produced which has been written by him making the libel, then the burden will be upon him to show that the letter is a forgery, or that it has been misinterpreted; or indeed that the relevant statement in the letter is true.

The meaning of all the words in an assertion must not be at all ambiguous. This can only lead to ineffective argument. If we take, for example, the subject, "management is a better profession than shop-keeping" we must ask ourselves what "better" means: does it mean more remunerative, or that it offers greater opportunities for leisure? There will have to be agreement on the meaning, or rather use, of the word "better" before sound argument can take place.

For sound argument, then, we must—

1. assure ourselves that the assertion can be proved at least approximately true or approximately untrue;

2. see to it that there is only one assertion;

3. remember that the "burden of proof" rests with the person making the assertion;

4. make certain that all words are precisely defined.

What Must be Proved?

We must next discover what must be proved in order to establish the truth of an assertion. A suggested method for doing this is to divide a sheet of paper in two—placing on the one side of the paper all the reasons *for* the assertion, and on the other side of it all the reasons *against* the assertion. Discovering any potential clash of opinion will show the speaker what he has to prove to win his case. Apart from this, examination of the conflict of opinion will also disclose any matters that can safely be admitted without weakening the argument. Though this is said, remember that there is no need to prove anything which is unnecessary to the success of the argument.

At times topics may be associated with the matter under discussion, but they may not be necessary to the assertion that is being made. These should not creep into an argument; every effort should be made to exclude them. Only a matter that ultimately advances one's case should be related; any other argument is simply wasted effort.

Once one is decided upon the issues of the argument, admitted all that can well be admitted, and emphatically excluded any matter not bearing directly on the argument, an appeal might be made to experience and reference might be made to authority.

The reference to authority must be quite definite; a single authority should not be quoted too often. It may be helpful to quote from an authority used by one's opponent.

If an audience is involved, the authority quoted must be acceptable to it. In the course of the argument one may have to convince an audience of the *relevance* of the quote and the authority.

Argument by Induction

If a person observes a large number of facts, and draws from these observations a general law, this is called argument by induction. Where all possible facts have been examined, the induction is said to be perfect. But if the induction is perfect there cannot really be any further argument. Therefore, inductive arguments are mostly imperfect inductions, used to emphasize, as well as possible, truths which possibly cannot be directly known. An imperfect induction would suggest a guess in regard to the facts which have not been examined. This guess is known as the inductive hazard. To lessen risk of error in taking this hazard one must assure oneself—

1. that the facts unexamined are few enough to allow the induction;
2. that the facts examined are fair examples of those which found the case;
3. that there are no known exceptions to the facts examined.

Argument by Analogy

Another form of argument, closely connected with inductive reasoning, is analogous argument. In analogy, instead of observing many cases, one compares the case in question with another case. One then concludes that because the cases being examined are alike in a number of particulars, they are probably alike in another. One must again assure oneself that the similarities of the two cases being examined are essential and that the facts on which the analogy is based are true.

Deductive Argument

In some areas of knowledge a definite law is discoverable. It is not necessary to prove individual facts in order to reveal this law. Where such law exists one may start with it, and apply the law to a particular case. It is necessary, once more, to be certain that both premises are true and that the conclusion stated in the given case is an instance of the established law.

Arguing from Effect to Cause

If a person sees car tracks leading up to his door, he may be reasonably convinced that someone has called. This may be said to be reasoning from effect to cause.

If the managing director of a large company falls seriously ill, and, following an announcement of his illness in the press, there is a decrease in the price of the company's shares, it may be reasonable to infer that the drop in the price of the shares occurred because of the illness of the managing director.

Argument of this kind is very common. But one often hears people, because, perhaps, of rumour, drawing conclusions from given events in a very haphazard way.

Care against a Mistake

Care should be taken to ensure that—

1. the alleged cause is not really simply another effect of the same cause;

2. the alleged cause is not associated with the known effect simply by chance;

3. the alleged cause was capable of producing the known effect.

Arguing from Cause to Effect

This is rather similar to the previous type of argument, but a person must be careful to make sure that the known cause is strong enough to produce the given effect. He must also make certain that the given cause will not be prevented from achieving its effect by some other cause.

Refutation of an Argument

If a person knows how to construct a good argument of his own, he naturally will notice his opponent's failure to do so.

If a person undertakes to refute an argument made by an opponent he should first of all decide what kind of argument he is attacking. We have examined four main types of everyday argument: argument by induction, analogy, deduction and from effect to cause or cause to effect. One should apply the tests already given for establishing a sound argument, whatever type it may be. For convenience, it may be well to summarize these tests.

TESTS FOR INDUCTIVE ARGUMENT

1. Has the person concerned examined enough examples to justify his assertion?

2. Were these examples fair?

3. Are there any exceptions which he may have overlooked?

TESTS FOR ARGUMENT FROM ANALOGY

1. Are the similarities of the two cases cited necessary for the particular case advanced?

2. Can it be said that the facts upon which the analogy is based are true?

TESTS FOR DEDUCTIVE ARGUMENT

1. Can the general laws cited be said to be true?

2. Is the assertion made in regard to the particular case true?

3. Is the fact alleged in regard to the particular case a known instance of the law?

TESTS FOR ARGUMENT FROM EFFECT TO CAUSE

Is the cause cited—

1. Merely another effect of the real cause?

2. Associated with the effect purely by chance?

3. Something that existed before the effect?

4. Something which can produce the effect?

TESTS FOR ARGUMENT FROM CAUSE TO EFFECT

1. Is the cause stated something which can produce the effect?

2. Is it not possible that some other cause may prevent the working of the argued cause?

Sometimes the arguments of one's opponent seem sound in themselves. This is only so if the facts upon which the arguments are based are true. The truth of the facts, however, on which the arguments may be based, are perhaps doubtful. Then it may be expedient to *test* the authorities used by one's opponent to support his facts.

Further Quotes

J. M. Keynes, speaking of causality, said: "We wish to know whether knowledge of one fact throws light of any kind upon the likelihood of another. The theory of causality is only important because it is thought that by means of its assumptions light *can* be thrown by experience of one phenomenon upon the expectation of another."

Professor Stebbing described causality as follows: "Daily experiences lead us, then, to distinguish between *what always happens and what sometimes happens but not always.* If we are successful to order our experience and to know what to expect, we must be able to replace *sometimes* by *always.*" We must be sure that any characteristics belonging to uniformities are quite different from multiformities. "There would be such an intrinsic difference if all uniformities were causal connexions. We have to inquire whether this is the case, and what precisely we mean by saying that a uniformity is a *causal* uniformity."

John Locke put the common sense view of causality this way: "We are wont to consider the substances we meet with, each of them as an entire thing in itself and independent of other things; overlooking for the most part, the operations of those invisible fluids they are encompassed with, and upon whose motions and operations depend the greatest part of those qualities which are taken notice of in them, and are made by us the inherent marks of distinction whereby we know and denominate them. Put a piece of gold anywhere by itself, separate from the reach and influence of all other bodies, it will immediately lose all its colour and weight and perhaps valuableness too; which, for aught I know would be changed into a perfect friability. . . . This is certain, things however absolute and entire they seem in themselves, are but retainers to other parts of nature for that which they are most taken notice of by us."

17 Education and Training
A Chapter on the Nature and Needs of Both Education and Training

"EDUCATION and training" has been the theme of many conferences. If a firm is at all concerned with the succession to responsibility in it, then it will be concerned very much with the twin concepts of "education" and "training," both in external courses and internally.

The two words, making one term, are similar but nevertheless quite different. Education describes, naturally, the process of educating, activating and disciplining the various powers of the mind, or instilling the principles of management as an art. It means the process of getting to know *what* skills are required in a job. Training describes the formulation and exercise of efficient techniques. More particularly, education and training include both information about the working environment, and also appreciation of the sources of information.

"Education and training" has been included in this book because effective communication accomplishes something at least of both education and training. Generally communication will enable people to exercise their minds more confidently and capably, and so enable them to become easily aware of the more efficient techniques.

Sending People on a Course

Any difficulty in sending people on a course, described as an education and training course, becomes peculiarly troublesome when the more mature manager is affected. This is partly because the term "education and training" has fallen very low indeed, and so has insufficient reputation to stimulate interest. Partly the reason is that external courses—those held at colleges and universities—although they have much to commend them, are of little practical value and interest. For one thing, technical training is better given within the company itself, where required tools and machines exist, than in a college or university.

If academic courses are aiming to attract senior and more mature managers, then the tutoring staff must also be senior with full and fairly long experience of industry. Students or delegates should be seen by someone responsible before the course in question begins, to get over that initial feeling of "going back to school." The course must finally be tailored to meet actual problems encountered by the people concerned. The problems will become clear at the initial meeting held with the students or delegates, whatever they be called.

An Education and Training Department

An education and training department must help a company to meet its obligations by providing well-qualified employees, at all levels, suited to present jobs and ready for potential advancement.

A distinction must be recognized, though not necessarily enforced, between formal and informal training and education. Formal courses relate to organized meetings for lectures or conferences or syndicate methods. Informal courses relate mainly to advice, and to the continuous responsibility of line authority both to train and to educate through *constructive supervision*, through really *useful instruction, informative order-giving* and *helpful criticism*. There should be no effort to remove this continuing responsibility from line personnel. The education and training department is a *service* organization, and so must encourage and aid line responsibility by providing improved facilities and better methods.

Formal courses are really supplementary to informal courses. The best education and training, both in skills and in attitudes is done on the production line.

Duties of an Education and Training Department

There are fifteen duties which a department of this nature should assume—

1. to survey the company and individual departments; and only on the basis of this survey to formulate a blue print of training or educational needs. These needs are not ends in themselves but means of meeting the company's obligations;

2. to help establish the broad policies of company training and educational programmes;

3. to help to organize departmental training and education when desirable; to help in formulating and maintaining standards of training and education for the guidance of individual departments;

4. to arrange the *company's* training and education courses to meet the *combined* needs of departments;

5. to give information and help on specific courses;

6. to provide outside help when it is required; to help in evaluation of such courses as may be held outside;

7. to provide course material for education and training;

8. to help in determining the most suitable method for selecting employees for courses;

9. to train company personnel in instruction techniques. Good instruction must be in accordance with principles of good teaching;

10. to be on call at all times for consultation and advice to all who enter a course; to keep executive management informed on the needs and achievements of the various departments;

11. to develop contacts with external associations and institutes in order to keep abreast of the latest techniques;

12. to develop all specialist courses such as apprentice training, supervisory training and executive development courses;

13. to follow up all education and training;

14. to enable the understanding and participation of executive management;

15. to keep the Board informed of progress through reports.

Considerations that Might Affect an Education and Training Policy

There are seven considerations relating to a training and education policy that must be borne in mind at all times—

1. no education and training course should be given unless there is evidence of a special need for it;

2. courses should be during working hours except in special circumstances;

3. courses should not use more than two hours of a participant's time per week;

4. all meetings should be arranged through a central service to make sure of the efficient use of time;

5. a training and education committee should review proposed courses and submit its recommendations. This committee should have production, engineering and staff representation;

6. all departments should have direct responsibilities in the establishment of any course, and co-operation should be maintained with these departments at all times;

7. when a special need for courses arises, senior management should express their approval.

EXPENSES

The training and education activity must try to earn at least its own cost by helping to improve production. In any event all such activity should be examined to see if it can justify the expense involved. Management must enable employees to attend courses, and charge for such time as they are away on formal courses.

Possible Education and Training Courses

1. Apprenticeship training and education;
2. induction courses;
3. operator courses;
4. supervisory courses;
5. executive courses;
6. office courses;
7. sales courses.

An examination of jobs is necessary before creating an education and training course for anyone. As Dr. Bakke put it: "Over-training, or training beyond the reasonable limits defined by the training need, is both wasteful and a source of poor morale and discontent (for example, it would be uneconomical to encourage twenty persons to take a course in tool design if present and future needs indicate a maximum utilization of ten tool-design trainees). A hope would have been installed in each person that, upon successful completion of the training course, a better job and higher pay perhaps might be forthcoming; and the disappointment that might follow when the majority are unrewarded and only a few are advanced would offset a great deal of the values derived from the course."

APPRENTICESHIP COURSES
There should be a distinction drawn between production courses and pre-production courses.

Pre-production
Any education and training given in pre-production is mostly a kind of induction activity, but it is also an elementary appreciation course on the general nature of tools and machines.

On-production

In this on-production activity, ordinary line personnel would give the necessary useful instruction or orders. Enlightened criticism will do the main education and training work on this occasion.

INDUCTION COURSES

Management has to accept that attitudes are controllable. Induction courses can help to form sound attitudes, to stop exploitation of uninformed minds, and generally to strengthen the communication between management and employee.

Induction courses should be designed to develop the process by which new employees become satisfied members of the company. The courses would cover various topics, and some of these might well be: a picture of products manufactured; company rules and policies; organization structure and services; social activity; chances for promotion; outside courses for apprentices; and so on.

OPERATOR COURSES

These courses should, in effect, help to reduce staff turnover, improve production, and encourage morale in the company by helping employees to adjust quickly.

In regard to these courses, the education and training department has the responsibility of helping departmental heads in the choice of suitable job instructors.

The important objective of an operators' course is to make available to all operators good instructors for the various departments to instruct workers in the best way of doing their work.

SUPERVISORY COURSES

The purpose of these courses is to help supervisors to handle well their human and production problems. It should so develop supervisors that they themselves produce a minimum of problems. The main purpose of a course is to prevent rather than to correct; supervisors are helped to recognize problems before troubles occur. The course should actually help them so to behave that fewer problems in fact arise.

Supervisor courses should distinguish between management courses and technical courses. The main objectives of management courses are—

1. to improve appreciation of human relations and of good supervision; to bring to the notice of supervisors a better understanding of their responsibilities and for them to appreciate ways of meeting these responsibilities;

2. to make supervisors aware of the problems of top management.

These courses should be contrasted with *pre-supervisory* courses. These latter courses are intended to establish capable and well-trained men to fill supervisory vacancies. These are helpful, although much of the desirable education and training should be exemplified by supervisors themselves.

Members of a pre-supervisory course would pay particular attention to order-giving, the handling of grievances and criticism. Cost control and waste would be a helpful addition to such courses.

All courses have to be realistic from the company's standpoint. Courses must be connected with the supervisors' problems at work. This may mean going to the operator and supervisory levels and examining what is happening, so that any subsequent discussion is developed within a realistic framework.

INTERNAL AND EXTERNAL COURSES

The stress should be on internal education and training, saving expenditure on the shorter conferences of management bodies and perhaps limiting external courses to residential or certificate work.

We have seen that education and training of supervisors is more efficient when rightly prescribed by line personnel.

13—(B.648)

The department of education and training may help to diagnose needs and prepare plans.

If possible, different managers within the organization should chair the different discussion sessions. These sessions should, apart from other benefits, enable supervisors to understand top management and its problems; it will enable, at the same time, top management to understand the supervisor and his problems. The objective of these discussion sessions will be—

1. to increase the supervisors' knowledge of the organization of a company and the work of departments other than their own;

2. to increase the amount of intelligent co-operation with other departments;

3. to increase the amount of personal contact between supervisor and manager.

EXECUTIVE COURSES

The education and training department should make available to management groups the latest information available to management. The main advantage here is for management groups to meet and to pool their knowledge and experience in discussion. The main objective of such meetings would be to discover new and improved methods of dealing with human and technological and organizational problems.

No reference has been made to training and educating for succession, although all such courses are in their proper sense "training for succession." It is impossible to make any recommendations for such education and training unless there is a definite company policy on succession.

Regarding courses for existing managers, the discussion group is again the most useful medium. Under the guidance of the discussion leader, six or seven members of management could meet to discuss some management thought and practice, interchanging knowledge and experience of a particular task. This type of meeting is similar, in effect, to the formal lecture or conference technique.

OFFICE TRAINING

The education and training department should offer courses containing instruction for section heads, clerks, secretaries and typists. The main objective of this course would be to bring to the notice of office employees any practices and techniques suitable to office procedure. The emphasis would be on the development of effective office supervision.

SALES TRAINING

The education and training department might arrange occasional meetings for members of the sales force, both in the field and in offices. Apart from examining their own practice, salesmen might be encouraged to examine sales promotion practices.

POTENTIAL OF COURSES

All courses have both a short-range and a long-range potential. The short-range purpose is to make a man better at his job at the present time. The long-range purpose is to regard each member of a course in the light of his potentialities as a possible candidate for promotion.

18 Postscript

A Chapter Devoted to a Restatement and Summary of the Contents of this Book

WE outlined only some of the arguments on good communication. This by no means exhausts the very wide subject. It is hoped, however, that the outlines will give the right kind of provocation to more detailed thinking about communication. But thinking about the problem is more than mere intention. Intention is something which, in isolation, proverbially paves the way to hell.

There are many people in industry who know very much more about the problem of communication when actually acknowledged than the writer. This has been known throughout, but the outlines are an attempt to guide the more detailed consideration of the experienced.

Communication Theory

Theories of information and communication are mainly physical and mathematical in origin. They are concerned chiefly with the rate, range and form in which information can be given, whether to machines or to man. The information is then stored by machines or men so as to give the greatest probability of unambiguous transfer of information. The fact that information and communication theory in the technical sense rightly affects the whole problem of communication is no excuse for the lack of its consideration by management.

Effective communication will influence particular functions, such as perceiving, thinking and motivation. Any social system—and an organization is a social system—is a system of roles, each of which has certain standards of performance and attitudes attached to it. Action will consist of the mutual adaptation of individual behaviour; it is important for such behaviour to be well informed, for from the behaviour rises many expectations. No one would deny that the expectations should be well founded.

Insight and Knowledge

It has mainly been argued in this book that insight should be given into any situation calling for increased understanding or action. It does not matter whether the communication be written or spoken; it is of great importance that there be a constant addition of information.

Apart from the particular knowledge an employee may need, there is general knowledge of the industry which can and should be given to him. William Cowper said: "Knowledge is proud that he has learned so much, wisdom is humble that he knows no more." We do not want an attitude of defeatism and appeasement, certainly not an atmosphere of defensiveness and safety first. The potential wisdom of subordinates is often shackled by fear. This may well be, at least partly, because management has not invited the employee's participation in the formulation of orders and policies affecting him.

Good communication will combat stagnation and promote the flow of knowledge or information capable of affecting present and future efficiency. This flow of information will affect the progress of industry, and perhaps open the way to improvements both in products and operating methods.

The flow of information is not only downward, but upward. One need not expect the people down the line to produce ideas, although one will be surprised at the extent to which these are forthcoming; what one *does* expect at least is some reflection of feelings.

A great deal of information is circulated in printed form to large numbers of industrial personnel; but it requires time to read it. The busy executive, exercised over urgent decisions, is often not a great reader with the special skill of interpreting information for its relevance to his particular problems; so we must ensure that the right elements of it are in the right places and will result in the required action.

Theoretically, the work might be done by an information department; but information officers know that not all the information they circulate is used by a person precisely where it might have a good effect. The problem begins with getting the flow of information going; after that there is still the question of how to get it accepted. It is up to a manager to demonstrate that information exists, that it is needed, and that it can be put to use. We do not wish a subordinate to be a type of domestic pet, who will do things he is told to do without question; who has the *practice* of doing a thing either automatically or in obedience—without ever thinking of an alternative suggestion. Effective communication will provide a means of ensuring participation, in thought at least, at the right levels.

Communication and Attitudes

The oral communication of ideas and information remains the most important of all forms of contact between individuals. Oral communication makes a great impression and can lead to thought and action.

What is needed for self-confidence is a feeling both of accomplishment and success. This may require—

1. a clear goal;
2. a sense of community in the attainment of the goal.

Communication, apart from its informative effect, will promote the right kind of attitudes towards people and towards the work being done. It will establish both the goal and the sense of community. It will develop a team spirit, and an awareness that others are motivated as oneself, and will thus encourage an appreciation of other people's work.

Communication will develop an attitude of mind which should make tasks lighter, because it will make comprehension easier.

Unless a person has satisfaction and even pleasure in doing a job then that person will not, with the best intention in the world, develop as a successful and worthwhile employee of an organization. He will at best continue, if he does at all, because of the money. But we have already considered the point that people should feel pleasure and satisfaction, and this not merely because they are human beings; even if we are cynical and are concerned solely with the progress of our business, it is necessary that employees feel thus if they are to give full value for their wage or salary. The argument we examined was that we are failing in a managerial responsibility if we do not succeed in establishing an employee's pleasure and confidence. The more sensitive and the more intelligent people become, the easier our task will be but, the argument ran, if we want them to be more sensitive we must inform them more.

In informing people we are carrying out the task of helping management to produce able successors. If we leave them requiring information which we never give, it will not be a long time before they become mediocre, without the desire to rise above that mediocrity. Even if we look at the matter selfishly, we are complicating the tasks of management.

Where communication falls on ears that will not listen, or do not listen well, the fault is more often to be found in the communicator than in his subordinate.

We cannot create a new attitude in a person except by working in the terms of the attitudes that already exist. So often (too often) many people in a position of command are unaware of existing attitudes, doubts and anxieties. The possibility of adaptation, for example in the training of staff to implement a particular policy, is simply nil.

Organization—Creation

The *creative* forces of any organization need an atmosphere of freedom, one in which employees may feel free and not be suffocated. An organization should *give an individual free access to ideas*, from superiors and subordinates as well as from those on an equal level.

The organization should be something that brings together a variety of backgrounds and experiences. If the view of an organization is: "We don't tolerate mistakes," then many useful ideas will be left untried.

For progressive policy is something that encourages venturesome thinking, appreciating that good ideas will contribute enough to outweigh bad ones. There may yet exist a certain approach in policy and procedure that may hinder creative thought of this kind. A policy of this kind arises frequently from the attitude, "We have always done it that way; so it must be the right way." The custom of asking questions, and even doubting their validity or relevance should be recognized.

Sanctions

At one time in industry, giving instructions or orders was comparatively easy. It was, in fact, easy to be a manager. One simply instructed or ordered people to do a thing; if they did not obey immediately they were sacked because there was someone else waiting to get the job. That does not happen any more. The sanction behind an instruction or order has changed.

The sanctions behind orders are different today from what they were in the past. We can no longer *make* people work, we must seek to make them *willing* to do so.

Why does a person obey an order? Does he obey because he is frightened? Does he obey because his wage packet depends on obedience? Does he obey because he is loyal to the company? Does he obey because he respects the person giving the order, or because he believes in the orders given to him? The latter answer reflects the basis of good management. People should obey because they respect and believe.

Understanding the Nature of Communication

Understanding *how* to communicate well is as important as understanding *what* one should communicate. The principles of good communication must be regarded as part of management's practice throughout each day, and so be merged into daily routine activity.

Good communication will not remedy all discontent. It will, however, create that sense of participation necessary to loyalty and good works relations; for their appeal is not only to better understanding but to sympathy as well.

Where people of different interests try to communicate, serious misinterpretations can easily result. This is what may happen where both sides are being honest, and are trying to get their ideas across effectively. Industrial relations are exacerbated, with no conscious intention on either side. This deterioration of feeling is largely accounted for by undefined language.

Defined language

On one occasion a farmer saw an artist painting on a canvas. The farmer said to him: "You are resting, I see." "No," said the artist, "I'm working." A little while later the farmer saw the artist digging in his garden. "Now you are working," said the farmer. "Ah, no," said the artist, "now I'm resting from my work." It is this kind of misunderstanding that is the cause of much industrial strife.

Supervisory Practice

Differences in evaluation occur particularly in supervisory activities and personnel work. These differences can be a serious obstacle to common understanding even though both sides are being objective. A supervisor, for example, in a chemical plant handed a mixer to a worker and said to him: "Give it a good hard tap." The supervisor was infuriated to see the bottom of the mixer smashed by the new worker. The supervisor was a slim, delicate man using chemical scales carefully. The worker was large and powerful. His idea of a "hard tap" was hardly that of the supervisor's. The supervisor would communicate well if he said, "Tap it as hard as *this*." The value of the word should be thus clearly shown.

The lesson for management is plain: it should keep intended values related to the real world. If management were careful about the potential danger of ambiguous evaluation, the habit of definition would at least minimize the dangers.

The principal ground of misunderstanding lies in the different evaluations which have been "learned" from past experience. If there is a considerable difference in past experience, which is inevitably the case, misinterpretation is bound to occur.

We are inclined to assume similarity of experience, especially among those who have risen from the ranks. With differences of experience this can be a very unwise assumption to make. It is especially dangerous when regard is had to the fact that experience is related to the development of attitude. As Stuart Chase once said: "Words are words and things are things. They are related only as we ourselves relate them. And each of us may relate them differently."

The assumed relations between words and things is one of the chief causes of communication failure. We tend to believe that words signify the same things to others as they do to us.

Line Management and Communication

Good communications do support and strengthen any sound organizational system, but, if the system is to be strengthened, line management must do the communicating job. Having the greatest opportunity for face-to-face contact it should develop an ability to communicate well.

There must be a desire to communicate as much as possible with employees. This will mean listening to the employees with every effort to understand their attitudes, what they require and what is of concern to them. The need for effective communication in line management is clear when one is aware, as Dr. Bakke has said, that "a person sees things as he is, not as things are . . . he listens to what is said but seldom hears what is meant." The onus upon line management to speak effectively, and to use language well, becomes a necessary function and not purely a matter of Christian charity.

Though a manager may believe he listens carefully, he may well not discern the meanings behind a person's reactions. He must guard against a natural tendency to be overhasty in judging, approving or disapproving. Intelligent listening and intelligent questioning are important aspects of good communication.

Management has much to learn from this practice of adaptation. On one occasion discussion was held with some workers representing about twenty-five major companies. The discussion was on the relationship between the workers and supervisors. One worker said: "There is a certain man in our company whom we respect for his ability, judgement and experience, but when he comes up to talk to you he fair gives you the creeps." He was asked what he meant by that, and he answered: "I am doing a job and this man approaches, hands in pockets, swaying on the heels of authority; then he lifts a hand and starts to speak. By the time he has got his mouth open I am unwilling to listen to him."

Language

The study of language is a discipline in fields of thought which, until now, have not acknowledged that this study had any significance for them. A consideration of the function of language is long overdue in the field of industrial administration and relations.

This is important in view of a growing management jargon, most of it indefensible and useless. This jargon is leading to increasing dangers and futile talk or misunderstanding—often more energetic than useful. The technique of using language well is, in the last resort, the technique determining most other techniques.

No one will doubt that it should be a cardinal principle of communication for a speaker or writer to use language which his listeners or readers can understand. The "operative" word is understand. Our concern is for those methods of using language which will make that understanding doubly sure. The spadework of linguistic definition cannot easily be avoided, even though this may be a source of worry.

The problem of "meaning" can be seen in this story from *Punch*—

Townsman: (On a visit to the country) pointing to molehills: "What are those?"
Farmer: "Them be oompty-toompts."
Townsman: "What are umpty-tumpts?"
Farmer: "Oompties made by the toompties."
Townsman: "But what *are* tumpties?"
Farmer: "Why, them what makes the oompties, you fool."

Words are precision tools to be used effectively in the daily conduct of business.

We cannot say that language does not have intense inward insight and experience. It certainly carries at most times both insight and experience. But the fact remains, that, when giving an instruction, we simply have to engage in the tiresome business of definition, to make sure that people will act properly and competently in the required sense.

Meetings

We examined the character that meetings should develop. Unfortunately, meetings as at present conducted are an obstruction, rather than a positive help, to good relations. This is evident for a number of reasons, but mainly because management and employees are so reluctant to have more meetings. If meetings develop the character advised, they will prove to be among the best of the forms of communication. They will not only enable an easier and better flow of information, but they will also help to make joint consultation much more effective.

Meetings are not popular at the present time because those who attend them do not believe that they have any value. A shop steward on one occasion was overheard to say: "I am sick and tired of the average meeting as conducted by an incompetent chairman. I know we have 'lobbied' for the meeting; but management, although members of it may use a different term, has 'lobbied' too; certainly members have made up their minds what they intend to say. There is no one in the chair to ask appropriate questions and to summarize the answers to them. Everybody attends the meeting in a spirit of debate, each side attempting to assert what it believes.

"The practice of counting hands instead of judgements is fatal. I can remember meetings occurring in exactly the form they now have about thirty to forty years ago, and probably meetings will be the same forty years hence. No wonder there is the tiresome repetition of the same old actions—banning of overtime, walk-outs, etc."

The argument is that meetings must really become far more alert and effective. We cannot afford to remain shackled to procedural forms that have no application to the kind of meeting we normally run or attend.

This book has emphasized ability in a leader, and not merely functional rights, since good meetings lead to a happier and more effective performance.

Joint Consultation

If meetings are to develop a character recommended, then joint consultation will not only be more efficient in itself but will promote the kind of communication we have been talking about.   The joint consultative committee can be used to a far greater extent than it has been.

Talking of joint consultative committees, we must face the fact that unofficial strikes often occur because workers are unwilling to attend their own branch union meetings, and so to elect the right people to represent them.   Most workers stay away because the avid committee member develops a kind of committee jargon unattractive to the worker who is unwilling to attend and listen to procedural argument.

Many of the divisions among unions are the result, less of deliberate intention, than of the barriers created by language. Of course there are sources of difficulty other than linguistic. Many of the restrictive practices on both sides of industry cannot be explained away by simple reference to word difficulty.   Nevertheless language does play proportionately too large a part.

Agenda and Minutes

The main stress was on the asking of questions in agenda. The minutes, it was said, should contain statements of the accepted summaries of the chairman.

Effective Speaking

Effective speaking becomes a matter of great importance to those concerned with establishing harmonious relations and co-operation.

We have observed that all speaking requires at times a precision, together with a knowledge of how evaluations are made.

Very frequently an order is given behind clenched teeth, and especially in a noisy shop it is almost impossible to hear what the person is saying. As we have the *onus* of creating sympathy and receptivity, it devolves especially upon us to speak audibly if we are to be listened to at all.

While there may be every excuse for a "backroom boy" to be inaudible in speech, there is no excuse when other people are vitally affected.

The greater the fluency with which a person can talk in public, the more likely he is to talk clearly when occasion demands. Not being hamstrung by copious notes or some other aid to memory, a manager need concentrate very little on putting things across. He will regard clear speaking a part and parcel of his functions.

Talking is a perfectly natural activity until we begin to think about it; it then becomes complex and troublesome. The familiar act of talking becomes strange and difficult as soon as one becomes conscious of it. Frequently a person on a public platform develops this kind of unfamiliar self-consciousness. People in the audience become uninterested or bored, and the speaker finds himself unable to say clearly what he means and as a result his thoughts become confused. The inclination then is to blame the audience. This may be an effective consolation for the ego, but will hardly help the speaker.

Talking and writing go together. Writing is simply representing on paper the things we say. Consequently the more we develop good habits of speaking, the more our writing will improve, apart from the fact that we shall become more effective and influential.

Many business executives and professional men are seeking command of the technique of talking effectively, not only on public platforms but at intimate meetings of small groups. These people are seeking to improve their abilities, not only as public speakers, but as conversationalists and discussion leaders.

Purposes

We always speak in public for one or more of a number of purposes. We may intend to inform our listeners by adding to their facts and ideas, or by strengthening their judgement. We may wish to entertain or delight the person or persons we are speaking to; we would then concentrate on narrative or dramatic means or perhaps descriptive means. We may wish to arouse a person or persons to praise or blame. We may wish to convince a person or persons of the truth or falsity of an idea or of behaviour. We may wish to stimulate reflective thinking on a problem, or to persuade people to follow a given course of action.

It is when we are *informing* people, convincing them of truth or falsity, or stimulating them to reflective thinking, that *definition* becomes necessary. There is no intention that one should do a Dr. Joad and say: "It all depends what you mean by . . ." It would be unreal to urge a constant linguistic perfection throughout a busy day. At the same time, however, we should be aware that many of the industrial aggressive actions stem from misunderstanding rather than malice.

In speaking to people not only are our words listened to but, of course, the manner and tone in which they are uttered affect the degree of attention paid to what we say. Manner and tone may even affect the interpretation of our words. Expression and demeanour are quite as significant as words themselves. Expression, tone and demeanour are often responsible for creating attitudes hostile to, or defensive against, the things we say.

We have emphasized that there is no magic about efficient speaking. Constant practice is the secret of the desired fluency. To learn to talk better and to get better reactions to the things we say we do not require a long treatise or course of instruction: the development lies in practice.

Often a would-be speaker is a member of an audience at,

for example, a conference. It would be a good thing for him to ask questions, and generally to speak from the floor whenever he can. People are apt to be deterred by this kind of practice, more especially when occupants of the front rows turn their heads around to get a better view of the person speaking.

Human Relations

We discussed the difficulty of "human relations." This is the most important of the matters affecting management. If human relations are to be effective to the full, employees will require to have a suitable range of basic satisfactions from their work.

Different kinds of companies will emphasize different aspects of "human relations," and within a particular company the factors of *desired* industrial behaviour should be examined at all levels, from chief executive to worker. We would then obtain a view of the overall picture of human relations at all levels. This will be possible mainly through a close study of the work situation.

Instructions

A dictionary defines instruction as the act of informing a person's mind or "to enlighten; to teach; to lead in the right way; to guide; to direct."

If instructions are given properly, they will enable that insight into the physical operations of a job which will ensure its competent performance. Instructions or order-giving are normally left to the ingenuity of foremen and chargehands without a special form of training. But these are among the most difficult of the forms of communication, and they certainly cannot be left to chance.

14—(B.648)

Letters

We also examined some of the rules for letter-writing. As speech came before writing, dictation of a letter is of special importance. It is possible to dictate with spontaneity without restricting clarity. Dictating, and consequently writing, well is a matter of inculcating good habits. The onus upon us all is to exchange bad habits for good ones.

The clarity we all intend is often hindered by pompous and absurd business phrases. Business phrases are unfortunately common in the teaching of letter-writing, and indeed it may have been at one time—now long past—fashionable to use these absurd phrases.

It is true that every writer has his own individuality and every business its own preferred style. The essence of any letter, however, lies in its freshness. Business jargon can succeed (if it succeeds in anything) only in complicating the problems that a letter might have. Jargon is, in any event, inclined to have a suffocating effect. Whilst one appreciates that certain difficulties will stand in the way of the inexperienced, both in writing and in dictating, these inexperienced people can be warned at least to watch carefully the beginning of their letters and the end of them.

Writing a letter well depends on being natural and dignified without being affected. If we are to clear our ground for good writing, then we have to be sure that our grammar and punctuation (which are really the good manners of words) are clear in our minds. We have to bear in mind here the relation of literary English to non-literary English. We are not concerned now with literary English, which has its own rules. Our main concern at present is with the use of non-literary English, and this demands that we should be as precise as possible at all times.

A good letter is important to a firm. It is not only a most efficient messenger, but is a very effective public relations servant.

Reports

We have seen that if a report is submitted, it should so pre-pare the reader or readers that they are better able to understand the information given to them.

The report-writer is concerned with the expression of scientific or technical facts and knowledge, and with the expression of judgements. He has a motive when writing, namely: to influence a manager's judgement or decision. So what he writes has to be *read, understood* and *acted upon* immediately. There is no time for a guess at possible meanings and implications. These must be quite clear to the reader.

A report-writer is writing within an industrial context, and not merely giving utterance to his own thinking. What is particularly important to him may be less so to the industry as a whole.

The general manager of a factory once pointed to a pile of reports before him, and said emphatically: "These reports are the only return the company has for money expended on the writer, and I can't read them—at least with the ease and convenience and understanding I should." Subsequent work with the writers revealed that they had little awareness of their need to write within a business context.

There is, as we have seen, a tendency to over-use technical vocabulary. John Locke rightly commented: "Vague and insignificant forms of speech, and abuse of language, have so long passed for mysteries of science; and hard or misapplied words with little or no meaning have, by prescription, such a right to be mistaken for deep learning and height of speculation, that it will not be easy to persuade either those who speak or those who hear them, that they are but the covers of ignorance and hindrance of true knowledge."

Scientific verifiability rests on the observation of facts, not upon accumulation of judgements. A report must—

1. be verifiable;

2. try to avoid inferences; very often we make an inference from observable facts. To say of a person "he was angry" is an inference, not a report or statement. The inference may be quite safe, but we must remember that it is an inference;

3. keep personal feelings out, try to avoid "loaded" words;

4. avoid slanting. Very often, although a report writer tries to keep judgements out, some nevertheless come in by implication.

Even when we use impersonal language we cannot get impartiality without difficulty. If we are aware of the feelings that certain words can arouse, we might be able to control our words to assure ourselves of sufficient impartiality for practical purposes. Sufficient awareness of our use of language will lead to a balance between favourable and unfavourable judgements. Selecting facts favourable to the subject or unfavourable to it is a form of slanting.

Practice in writing reports will improve our powers of observation. We shall recognize it in others and assure it in ourselves.

Interviewing

We stressed some of the major disciplines that should exercise us in a successful interview. There was no duplication of known techniques, but at the same time it is well to be agreed about the fundamentals of sound interviewing. Interviewing is a very important form of general communication, and is something that should not be left merely to the inspiration of the moment and without careful preparation.

Perhaps the most important of the forms of interviewing is the "counselling interview" which probably takes up a good proportion of a manager's time. The "counselling interview" affords endless opportunities for goodwill in advising an employee on his direction, and perhaps on the opinions held of him by others. When one considers that the average employee spends more time in a factory than with his own family, a "counselling interview" can be seen as a most important event to him.

"Counselling" was originally an American development, and a certain amount of caution is necessary about its practice. The main function of counselling lies in "reflecting" the interviewee's emotions back to him, and allowing him to clarify his own phrases.

Some interviewers in general interview oppose all statements, with the result that the interviewee exaggerates all the more in an attempt to justify himself or his argument. To tell a person one does not believe he is being reasonable is most unacceptable to him if tension is at all present.

Reflecting the interviewee's reasons and emotions back to him will enable him to lose any sense of tension; he will then be able to see his emotions and statements in their true light.

An interview is the most effective means of discovering an actual or would-be employee's attitudes. It is probably impossible, however, to establish what a person's *temperament* might turn out to be. It is often difficult to assess how a person will respond to obstruction, although psychological testing may help in this regard.

Delegation

The relation of both instructions and orders to delegation is obvious. We examined the concept of delegation in two of its connotations—

1. the appointment of a representative;
2. entrusting a group of people to the care and management of someone else.

Delegation, as has been said, is generally not well done. Once again it is left too often to a manager's discretion. Delegation should be regarded as so important that higher

204 / The Art of Communication

management must assure itself that delegation is taking place and that it is functioning effectively. Responsibility being a matter of moral attitude as well as something expressed in action, it is not possible to display it effectively without specific delegation.

Although delegation should be an obvious exercise in management, often managers do not delegate or delegate badly. We looked at delegation in both the sense of representation and as a responsibility discharged regarding our own subordinates.

The important thing in the delegation of responsibility is to maintain and enlarge the morale and encourage positive attitudes. Delegation, apart from its need to be framed in a helpful and positive manner, is at once an expression of responsibility and helps to create it.

The manager who delegates well makes his own task of management very much easier.

If delegation is to be entirely successful, the period of *accountability* must be clearly known. Very often a supervisor will go to a manager for advice, and the latter will say to him: "I entrusted you with authority, why do you come to me over every little thing?" The supervisor then often feels that he has to take his own decisions, and the manager says to him: "Why did you not come and see me to obtain the necessary advice?" The supervisor cannot possibly decide whether or not he should go to his manager. When accountability at regular periods exists, reporting back becomes easier for both the supervisor and the manager.

Enthusiasm

We dealt with "enthusiasm" and the importance of maintaining it in ourselves and encouraging it in others. This is an important matter if we are to maintain our position with increased competition; but although enthusiasm is a valuable quality, it is often overdone and needs a great deal of caution in its use.

It remains important, however, that people exercise every intelligence and capacity in anything they do.

A firm may be technically well organized, but that organization has to take note of effective social organization. This, of course, means more than creating an atmosphere of amiability; it means making use of the loyalty and goodwill to be found in almost every man and woman.

Our *egos* demand that we blame the people we control. By doing so our *egos* are content, but we may lose the opportunities we have for devleoping goodwill and loyalty.

Sound Argument

We examined the purpose and meaning of good argument. It becomes a matter of practical value to be able to conceive tests and to be able to apply them to the arguments before us.

It is certainly important as part of speaking well to argue positively. Apart from this, the ability to sum up a person's type of argument and to determine the tests applied to establish its validity sets a very good example. People are quick to notice any logical ability when it is called for.

Modern Management

What is most important in a manager are not only certain characteristics of personality and the requisite method of approach to particular problems, but the acquaintance at least with certain areas of generalized knowledge and with certain techniques used in the actual process of managing.

Business management is a vital function. The success or failure of our industrial management will probably affect the lives of many people, apart from management's own employees. Management has really become the most important activity of any industrial society. It is ultimately responsible for the economic stability for which every society aims. And without economic stability there can be no proper policy of social reform in one's own country or effective action abroad.

Not only must a modern manager be intelligent and vital, but he should possess an ability to communicate well; this, not only in issuing orders, but in the essential details of a situation, securing willing co-operation at all levels.

The manager has contact with groups of such widely differing social backgrounds and education, that it is not easy to communicate without showing condescension.

Good communication will in the long term produce a more efficient management. Not all, it is true, but at least some of the bad industrial relations lie in failure to maintain an effective communicative link and so avoid the infamous results of the guessing game.

Clearly, any giving of ideas from sources outside one's daily contact will develop the abilities expected from one.

It is difficult in the last resort to maintain an alert and receptive mind, and therefore a lively intelligence, without replenishing one's reserves in this way.

The Duke of Edinburgh, in an address to the National Union of Manufacturers, said: "We have now in this country to live by the wit of the scientist and the engineer, who by their inventions start new industries; by the wit of the specialist and the expert, who can improve the methods of production and materials; by the wit of the designer who can improve the product itself and its saleability. Finally and probably most important, we must exploit the wit of the manager. He is the co-ordinator who alone can bring together and make the best use of the ideas of the scientist, specialist and designer. The manager should be the great brain-picker, constantly on the lookout for new methods and new ideas."

Appendix

Education and Commerce

Technical and Commercial Colleges and the Art of Communication

IT may seem an impertinence to suggest that schools and colleges are not doing all they might do to develop (a) an understanding of, and (b) an ability in, the arts of communication. The loud complaints, however, of managements in industry and commerce about the incompetence of communication activity in their organizations do lead one to infer that there is a failure somewhere in the educative process.

One good answer to such a ready inference may well be that a systematic study of communication is a mature study; that it demands levels of knowledge and experience which make it inaccessible to other than well-educated minds. This is true when one thinks of communication theory or information theory, to which so many intellectual disciplines—including engineering, mathematical and statistical theories of information—have contributed.

But communication must be thought of in the more obvious, simpler sense of the term: namely, (a) the transmission and reception of oral and written messages (e.g. interviews, letters, reports, instructions, meetings) relating to everyday business activity; (b) the exchange of information and ideas, and controversy, in general social intercourse. In this sense, young people can at least be taught to use language with intelligence and discrimination, and be given some training in the effective presentation of oral information.

Even within this relatively limited meaning of the term "communication," the implications of the problem are wider than is commonly supposed. Their significance certainly extends beyond the practical demands of industry or commerce. They are significant for the whole field of human relations. Indeed, successful communication is fundamental to satisfactory human relations. The importance of the problem cannot be exaggerated. The problem of communication must go further than a division of it (with separate treatment) into letters, reports and public speaking. These applications in themselves call for patient study and improvement; but they cannot be isolated from one another. Nor can they be intelligently considered without regard to coherent, *general* principles—principles fundamental to *all* forms of statement or expression designed to achieve an intended result. Training in fluency is not enough.

People with a serious communication function must know something of *the processes of the communicative act* as such.

Within the scope of this short appendix, it is not possible even to begin to deal with the more subtle processes involved in even the simplest forms of human communication. Some of these processes may occur to mind if we ask ourselves the kinds of questions that may be typified as follows—

1. What establishes coherence? What makes writing and speaking thorough in relation to one's listener and reader? How is it best to emphasize the important and to minimize the unimportant? What in writing should decide the pattern of sentences and paragraphs, and the flow of ideas, always bearing in mind the need for adjustment to the capacities and interests of the readers?

2. What are the different kinds of discourse? Which is the most suitable for particular occasions? Where hostility

and suspicion exist, how shall we, at the same time as we inform, mollify hostility and allay suspicion?

3. What is the relationship between argument and conflict? Can argument within consultative committees attain to the status it deserves, and be recognized as something subject to quite objective rules in the conduct of discussion?

4. What is the influence of tone of voice and demeanour as the expression of attitudes and the qualification of meaning? How many undesirable moods do we create, less because of what to say than the way we say it?

5. How far do we consciously control our language and how far are we controlled by it? To what extent does language restrict our own thinking, apart from our communication with other people? What are the different effects and dangers of colloquial, informed and formal or technical language? How do words come to derive connotations so different from the sense we intend them to have, and how do we guard against this danger?

All these questions are really part of two basic queries which should be asked—with an attempt to find the answers —by those people intending to attain to positions of responsibility in industry or commerce—

1. How can I make it reasonably easy for people to read or listen to what I have to say?

2. How can I communicate most effectively in order to inform, and in order to reduce the scope of ambiguity, misconception, tension and resentment?

Judging from the complaints of industry and commerce, the questions are not asked or the answers are not sought.

The major part of an educative process should be—

1. consciousness of the deficiencies of language and of the dangers of misunderstanding;

2. a determined effort towards effective communication;

3. a determination to distinguish between *evaluative* and *referential* speaking or writing;

4. consciousness of, and willingness to re-examine, one's own assumptions.

We have already spoken about S. I. Hayakawa and Stuart Chase. Use of these books in colleges will be of great value. Hugh R. Walpole's *Semantics* deals with the nature of words and their meanings and might well be prescribed. It contains some valuable practical exercises which a student is well suited, or should be, to do himself.

Bibliography

CHASE, S., *The Tyranny of Words* (London, Phoenix House, 1955)

ELBOURNE, E. T., *Fundamentals of Industrial Administration* (London, Macdonald and Evans, 1941).

FLESCH, R., *The Art of Plain Talk* (New York, Harper and Brothers, 1946).

HAYAKAWA, S. I., *Language in Thought and Action* (London, Allen and Unwin, 1956).

HUNTER, G., *Studies in Management* (University of London Press, 1961).

KAPP, R. O., *The Presentation of Technical Information* (London, Constable and Company, 1942).

MAIER, N. R. F., *Psychology in Industry: a Psychological Approach to Industrial Problems* (Boston, Houghton Mifflin, 1955).

NELSON, J. R., *Writing the Technical Report* (New York, McGraw-Hill, 1952).

OGDEN, C. K., and RICHARDS, I. A., *The Meaning of Meaning* (London, Routledge, 1949).

OLDFIELD, R. C., *The Psychology of the Interview* (London, Methuen, 1941).

OVERSTREET, H. A., *The Mind Goes Forth* (London, Jonathan Cape, 1956).

SMITH, M., *An Introduction to Industrial Psychology* (London, Cassell, 1943).

STEBBING, L. S., *A Modern Introduction to Logic* (London, Methuen, 1950).

STEBBING, L. S., *Thinking to Some Purpose* (Harmondsworth, Penguin Books, 1939).

THOMSON, R., *The Psychology of Thinking* (Harmondsworth, Penguin Books, 1959).

THORNDIKE, E. L., and GATES, A. I., *Elementary Principles of Education* (New York, A. G. Seilar, 1929).

TRELEASE, S. F., *How to Write Scientific and Technical Papers* (Baltimore, Williams and Wilkins, 1958).

VALENTINE, C. W., *Psychology and its Bearing on Education* (London, Methuen, 1960).

WALPOLE, H. R., *Semantics* (New York, Norton and Company, 1941).

Index